CARPENTER MEMORIAL LIBR
Cle Elum, Washington 9892

The Wolf, *the* Woman, *the* Wilderness

The Wolf, *the* Woman, *the* Wilderness

A True Story of Returning Home

Teresa tsimmu Martino

NewSage Press

The Wolf, the Woman, the Wilderness
A True Story of Returning Home

Copyright 1997 Teresa tsimmu Martino
Softcover ISBN 0-939165-29-5
All rights reserved. No part of this book may be reproduced or used in any form or by any means without permission in writing.

Address inquiries to:
NewSage Press
PO Box 607
Troutdale, OR 97060-0607
503-695-2211
Fax 503-695-5406

Cover design & book design by John Rodal

Printed in the United States

Distributed by Publishers Group West
1-800-788-2123

Library of Congress Cataloging-in-Publication Data

Martino, Teresa.
The wolf, the woman, the wilderness : a true story of returning home / Teresa Tsimmu Martino.
p. cm.
ISBN 0-939165-29-5
1. Wolves—Puget Sound Region—Anecdotes. 2. Wildlife reintroduction—Canada. 3. Martino, Teresa. I. Title.
QL737 . C22M36445 1997
599. 773—dc21 96-45468
CIP

1 2 3 4 5 6 7 8 9 10

Dedication

For my family: Mother, Grandpa, Margaret, Marty, Lisa, Andrew, James, and the ancestors.

To the people of the island who gave me a place to live.

To my friends in Osage and Blackfeet and other Native nations who welcomed me back.

For Maureen and Susan and all who helped with this book, for M.A.K. and S.D.

To Mike the man who walked like a bear.

And to the wolf who has no name. May hunting always be good and may the seventh generation see your children.

Thanks Mystery.

Mckenzie

I know a wolf. She was born captive in the northern mountains, but her grandparents were free. I taught the wolf to return to her people. For a year we traveled between my cabin and the northern wilderness. And in that time I returned to my people. The circle comes around, and the wolf became my guide. Now my eyes are bright gold like the wolf's, my pupils narrow to a pin prick.

The animals can speak. The wild has not lost her voice, she is calling us. Her voice is in the howling of wolves. And the wolves say, Come home.

Teresa tsimmu Martino

Contents

Chapter One

Mother Wolf's Dream

A wolf leaps up, placing her saucer-size paws on the chain-link fence and looks me full in the face. Her claws are black as stones, thick fur between her toes. She is the color of milk that stands in a silver pail in the sunlight. A trace of smoke like a shawl of dark fur, lies across her shoulders. Her eyes are as golden as summer and into those eyes I fall. The wolf's gaze melts into softness. Saints and angels must have eyes like these.

The old woman beside me moves restlessly. "She knows you. They always know their own." I glance sideways, curiously, at the old woman, crooked like a broken branch. The little breeze lifts her hair, the color of blood and snow, and blows it around her face. I am surprised at her words. "What do you mean?" I ask. "Mother Wolf knows you. She knows you are a wolf." Turning back to those golden eyes, listening to the old woman muttering beside me, the wolf and I speak in silence.

There are stories that swim in my blood, I know this. But until this moment I had not drawn the breath of wolves down into my lungs.

The wind though, brushing my cheek many times, hints of deeper connections. But blood is there: legends from my Italian ancestors about a city built by twins who sucked at the teats of a wolf bitch; dust that covers the red skin of my other people whom I hardly know. They followed the Wolf Nation, hunted after antelope. Perhaps Mother Wolf sees these things in my eyes and follows the myth into my heart where she digs a deep den and howls to call the pack.

Small sounds come from the dark box in the corner of the wolf pen, slippery little whines. Turning away from Mother Wolf and staring into the darkness, the old woman gestures, leading my eyes towards the box. "Babies. She has two. I don't know what we can do with them. We are closing the rescue center and retiring."

In the opposite corner of the dark pen that holds new life lies a ragged pile of bony fur. I walk over and peer at it. "Father," she mutters softly. "He's dying." I turn from the pen confused, and look into the old woman's watery blue eyes. Mother Wolf leaps on the wire fence, snarling. Her teeth catch it and her jaws seek something to crush. Is she frustrated? Angry because I have turned away? Startled, I turn back to face her. Mother Wolf comes back to me and her eyes dissolve into mine. "What is Father Wolf dying from?" "They are very old. Both are first generation removed from the wild." "Like me," I say to the old woman, still facing Mother Wolf. "The cubs are like me. Second generation removed from the wild."

While hunting for dreams in the high north I came upon this rescue center, lured by an elk in a pasture behind a ten-foot-tall fence. I was driving to put distance between something that is hidden; restlessness, longing, and anger. The old people had set up their rescue center with the best of intentions. Things happen that spiral down to entrap. They ran out of money and strength for the work. They have rescued a variety of creatures, from elk and fox, to several big cats. Their tiger and African lion had been kept in the base-

ment of a house until the owner realized the cruelty and the danger.

The old woman shows me around the facility. The cages are small but the animals look healthy. We turn a corner and a lion faces me. His eyes are as yellow as sunflower petals, but not as soft. They glitter against a backdrop of rippled tawny fur. His tail twitches and he throws his stare like a lance. His eyes are not gentle with melting compassion like Mother Wolf. His fierce gaze prods the soul, asking for the give-away, my life for his. If the cage had opened like some great metal flower and the lion sprang out, there is no doubt that he would have killed and eaten me on the hard ground of the rescue center. If I had looked into his eyes as he leaped, I would have relinquished to his asking for the give-away. I would have understood as he pulled claws into me and turned my neck to his teeth. Such power lies in his stalking glance.

Next to his cage is a tiger. The tiger has the spirit of a Buddha. He leans on his cage wire like a lover. I stick my hand through and stroke his head and chin. His whiskers are like cactus spines, his eyes are calm. He is like a sweet uncle, absent for a long time, now returned to the family. What had the tiger experienced in that cellar? The old woman told me that when animal services gave the tiger and the lion to the rescue center they were skin and bones. The lion and the tiger—-everyone deals with captivity differently.

I watch the old woman butcher a deer and a young moose. Both had been hit by cars on the dirt roads bumpy and deformed by frost heaves. She swings the ax with wiry arms knotted like pale ropes. With great skill she cuts off their heads.

There are several rescue wolves here. One is black, almost to blue. His eyes are as fierce as the lion's. He holds no courtesy for me or the old woman who feeds him. His family has abandoned him. Wolves bond deep. Their hearts are pulled by ties of fidelity that are like the chivalry of tribe or clan.

The blue-black wolf will never forget his people or forgive his captors. One day he escaped from his human family and went to the neighbor's house and ate some ducks. For that, they abandoned him. What does this wolf think of at night? Does he dream of his human family? Does he bound towards them in his sleep with the generosity of soul that makes humanity look uncivilized?

Mother Wolf whines, a musical sound, and I push my fingers through the mesh and stroke the top of her nose. Her eyes shine through me like sunlight through green leaves. The sky becomes electric indigo behind them. When the old woman brings out one of the baggy warm wolf babies, there is nothing else to do but to take her softly into my hands, her furry form just fits. Mother Wolf paces, staring, her eyes pour gold down my back like honey. Wolf and horse bodies are more familiar to me than my own. When I draw with charcoal or paint, I struggle to remember how my own cheek curves around my face. But a horse or wolf, I know well. When they move, I feel their muscles slide under skin and my spirit settles down to nest within their flesh. The cub's eyes are as blue as the sky blown clear of clouds. In time, this will change. Her coat is a dark storm-gray. The white coat of her mother is dominant, and the old woman predicts that one day the wolf will be white.

"Take one of these cubs." The old woman stands in the thin wind grasping my hand. "Take one...."

Every decision moves you down the trail of life. Move this way and you die young, move that way and you increase somehow. Standing there facing that old woman it seems to be the most natural thing in the world to take the little wolf. While I hold the cub close, I search with the old woman for a crate to put the wolf in. The cub seems accepting of this, and unconcerned, gnaws my hand. When it comes time to leave, the old woman stands and waves from the road. I drive away with Mother Wolf's eyes nailed into my heart.

Mother Wolf's Dream

Driving south, I wind along the spine of the northern mountains pushed up by the arching of the earth's plates that rub against one another like great cats. The backbone of earth runs along North America like a bony saw. The spike heads of mountains poke up frosted over with wisdom and winter. Trees stand tall, comb the fair blue sky. Eagles fly, calling down their high screams. A moose with hair like dry bark that sprouts in scraggly patches, crosses in front of my Jeep. What appeared as a boulder becomes a bear. She sits on her haunches, paws in her lap. The northern people have come out to watch us pass through.

There is plenty of time on this journey to wonder about *who I am*. The road rises up and promises me news of identity but no signs say which way to go. I have learned to feel the blood pull from the center of my chest like a living compass; to trust the inner guide that points me in the right direction. Perhaps my upbringing has carried me to this place. A Native friend told me that we carry our ancestors on our backs. But I think perhaps they carry us. We are a little raft of living bone and tissue floating on a river of blood going where the current takes us, or paddling frantically upstream.

For hours the road whirls away under the Jeep tires. My mind migrates to the past. I see my father point at the osprey flying over a lake. Granny, now dust, runs backwards beside a creek, a butterfly sticks to her as if trying to bestow a blessing. Perhaps the benediction of butterflies is the gift of becoming something else. The past carries me, sometimes sadly but always with stories I recall of loved ones who are still dead but here. They are balanced somewhere between my ribs and my head. I know how the ancestors would have felt about the little wolf cub. They would have taken her in as well.

A small noise from the crate on the passenger seat calls to me. Pushing my hand into it, a tiny tongue licks quickly over my palm. I rub the little round body and give the nose a squeeze. Another sound splits the air, thin but harsh and abrupt. It is my second passenger in the shoe box on top of the crate—a tiny black fox. Both animals are ten days old. Orphans caught between the cage and the wilderness. The old woman told me the fox cub was rescued from a fur farm. He protests his captivity with squeaky and loud irritating sounds that fall somewhere between running a rasp over a dull edge of steel and the scream of a puma. The little gray wolf whimpers softly and I see Mother Wolf's golden eyes surrounded by wire mesh.

Loneliness. My father was sick for most of my teenage years. He finally died when I was nineteen. His death was the stab of a javelin. Fifteen years later and I have yet to pull that spear out. If I do, I might bleed to death. My mother lost much of her balance when Pop died. They loved each other. It was like losing them both. After a year she wrenched herself back to life.

Moments can suspend like sand in sea water. The rolling waves of what we call *now*. Sometimes, I hesitate on the trail of my life; one bare foot on the ground, the other caught in mid-stride. Pause and think in this moment. Am I happy or sad? Bored or excited? Afraid? *Feel.* If I cannot sense the javelin twisting, I will never know joy. One is the trail marker to the other and they speak to each other in a soft brush voice. I gave the rescue center money for the gray wolf and the fox. Unknowingly, I bought back my soul.

My home in the Northwest is a four-day drive from the rescue center. For hours at a time I drive and the babies bob in their boxes. When we stop for fuel, I mix up their mess of feed—diluted skim milk and canned meat—which they attack voraciously. When they are finished, they frantically search for more. Slowly, as we travel, they settle into the rumble, rumble

of Cherry, my red Jeep . They begin to warm up to me as they identify me as a relative.

Wolves are social animals, like human beings. I know this from close association with them. I have been a free-lance rescue worker for twelve years, and several wolves have lived with me. My first wolf was Peter, half timber wolf and half malamute and husky mix. Peter is big and joyous, the color of ashes on frost. He is still my close companion along with my dog, Beanie, a blue-gray wiemaraner. Beanie is my resolute dog soldier. Together, the three of us have worked the horse business. We began in Northern California, my first home. Through tapestry hills of ochre and emerald, Peter and Beanie ran horses with me, easily keeping up with my thoroughbreds. We went everywhere together, and still do. They live in the house. Peter sleeps on the floor, most of the time.

In those days, word got out that I had wolves. It was then that the calls began. People phoned to see if I would take their wolf. Wolves and wolf-dog mixes make terrible pets. They destroy everything. At that time, I lived in the country, so I saw no reason not to adopt them; and I could not bear the thought of them being killed. After Peter more wolves came. There was Pearly, an Arctic wolf who wanted to eat my dog Beanie; Curly, a timber-wolf cross who was blind in one eye because someone had beaten him so brutally; and Toaster, a kind and calm timber cross who was more dog than wolf. The adopted wolves became my family. I built a big pen and neutered the wanderers. Some I gave to people who thought they could care for them. Others stayed.

Now my newest and youngest wolf whines softly, calling me back to the road. I pull the cub from her box and set her on my lap. In the warmth she falls asleep. Slowly the surrounding terrain changes. The snow-covered peaks dwindle in the distance as we drive through the troughs scraped clean as if caught in the teeth of a great predator. Grass grows here, and round rocks drop from the mouth of primordial-compressed snow.

At dusk I look for a motel instead of camping because of the babies. Finally, one turns up by a lone truck stop. This is the kind of motel found only in the high north—where people talk to you openly and the smell of spruce wanders into all the rooms. I carefully hide the babies in my backpack as we walk to the room. Once inside, I set them up in the bathroom. The little fox can maneuver much better than the young wolf. The wolf cub is much more clumsy and less independent somehow. I name the fox Kip, after a fox in a short story by Farley Mowat. The story is about a Native man who had an Arctic fox as a friend, then later had to sacrifice him to save his family from starvation. An old dilemma for people who subsistence hunt.

Now, to find a name for the wolf cub. Names are important. What you are called can be what you are. A person should have several names throughout life, and a secret name as well. The old woman told me that the young wolf's grandparents had been captured out of the wild in the Mackenzie Mountains in the Yukon. Somehow that worked. Mckenzie, after the beautiful home of her ancestors. I choose not to use the spelling of the name of the white explorer Sir Alexander Mackenzie, partly because those mountains had other names long before he first saw them. But I like the sound of the word, Mckenzie. This becomes her first name. But already, I call her by her second name, Baby.

Blockaded in the motel bathroom, Mckenzie crawls to the towels on the floor and starts dragging them around in wolf-like fashion. Kip moves about managing to spread a small amount of dung into a large area. The voracity of their appetite is astound-

ing. Mckenzie straddles her dish with legs that can hardly hold up her plump body and gulps the diluted milk and shredded meat as if she has been starving. Kip is a bit daintier, but he stands in his saucer and smears the food over his body. When he is done his fur stands up in sticky spikes from coagulated food. When I rinse him off in the bathroom sink, he does not seem to mind much. Rubbing him gently with a towel till dry, I put him back into his shoe-box nest to sleep. I am afraid to leave Kip alone with Mckenzie because of the difference in their sizes. Kip, small enough to lie in the palm of my hand, weighs less than a pound, and Mckenzie is a plump five pounds or more.

I lie down and fall asleep. Two hours later Mckenzie is awake and hungry. Her noises drift through the room. When I open the bathroom door, she stands glaring at me. In that moment, for the first time, I realize the nature of Mckenzie the wolf; intense, commanding, and inquisitive. While I mix her food, she stumbles over to investigate my bare foot. The toes interest her the most and she gamely tries to remove my toe nails with her tiny sharp teeth, snarling. She squints her eyes tight for concentration. When I remove Kip from his box, he appears to be in a coma. But when he smells the food on my finger tips he wakes up. He tries to suck on my nose when I hold him at eye level. His little beady black eyes do not yet focus, but his round face is as cute as a toy. So went the first night. Every two hours I fed the babies.

The next morning rises around us like a hundred flags. The colors stand out on the tips of clouds flying before the breeze. The tops of the spruce trees wave gently and the murmuring beckons a reflective state of mind. Something hangs on wind. If I listen words and feelings might become clear. When I carry the babies outside, they drink the breeze down, sniffing it with great interest. The wind lifts the fur on Mckenzie's back as it slips through the slats of her crate. I pack the animals in the car and we head out.

Migration always eases my spirits. When we campaigned horses, each season of travel brought peace. Humans, like wolves, are creatures of the trail. Traveling is instilled in us from the beginning to save the land from too much use. Migration allows us to use different food supplies and improve our nutrition. It eases the burdens of parasites, and within territories, at least, probably cuts down on aggression. Perhaps that is why, when there is unrest, people move so much. Our bodies tell us that travel will save us. But now there is no place to migrate. Instead, we humans hide in our houses and we do not tell each other the truth.

Fences cut my vision. My eyes long for distances to spread out before me, easing my sight. In the north where people are few, your neighbors represent safety and companionship. When people get too crowded they build walls to keep each other out, as if sick of the sight of their own kind. When animals are in captivity and get too crowded, they sometimes kill each other. In the wild they can leave. If there is limited space and food supply, wolves have fewer cubs. The wild animals are wise.

Looking out the windows of the Jeep the land changes around us. Fir, alder, and dogwood replace the spruce of the high north. Instead of the high backbone of mountains, there are now tall solitary peaks, the volcanoes of the Pacific Rim. The volcanoes make me think of wolves. There is a gesture among wolves that shows acceptance of a higher ranking wolf's authority. The subordinate wolf turns and exposes his neck to the leader's teeth. It is subtle, performed gracefully and with mutual respect. Volcanoes represent earth's power. So I wonder, shall I expose my throat in the gesture of understanding the power of the land? Mentally I do. With this thought comes peace and I hear the breath of the world whisper, *I will always care for you, but there will be change.*

The air becomes brighter, the towns are closer together. The

day turns around and becomes evening. Again, we stop at a motel, but people talk less here. Morning comes and I still feel tired. I no longer want to drive. My shoulder hurts where it had once been dislocated from falling off a horse. I want the trip to be over, to be back on my Northwest island home. There is another day and a half of driving. The route through the land becomes drier. Instead of trees there is a vast grassland scratched by scraggly barbed-wire fences. In the distance lie more jagged mountains covered with snow.

When I stop for gas I am careful what I say about my traveling companions. People have strong feelings about wolves. It seems they either love them or hate them. I have shown my wolves to grizzled farmers who scratched their heads in wonder after a wolf crouched down and timidly sniffed their boots. The wolf, I believe, is our teacher. But the wolf is also in competition with people for the land, for the wilderness. Maybe that is why there is resentment. But I wonder, what do people want in the future? What is their vision? Will the world consist only of vast cities and factory farms? Will there only be pockets of wild animals preserved in parks and zoos? And if that happens, what will we become?

Once over the mountain passes where the trees cling to rocky ground, suddenly, Puget Sound lies before us like a sea of dark jade. There, across the water lies the island covered with thick fir trees. It looks like a whale asleep on the surface of cold water. As we take the ferry across the Sound, the babies are roused by the rich scents flying in the windows. The smell and sounds of the sea are mysterious, as if someone ancient is trying to talk to us. The swish-roar of the sea's waves echo in my veins.

Puget Sound, the younger brother of the ocean, lies inside the Strait of Juan de Fuca. I came to the island by chance. A homey resting place for hunters of dreams. The island's horse people gave me the work I know and I settled down to think things over. Contemplation is an important concept easily missed in the modern world. Things are not meant to shoot by like rockets. They are meant to move clop, clop, clop, like hooves on a hard dirt road while you sit bareback to figure out the trail. Maybe if I am still long enough, questions will rise up like trout after a May fly. Watch! Some of those flies have hooks. I challenge those questions. Till now I only had my knitted cross-country gloves to throw down in the face of what I do not know. But now, a new Guide sits next to me in a little crate. Yet, I still do not recognize her.

If I could reach out with my hand and think long enough, I know I could peel back reality like the skin of a grape. But what would I find? I want to know! Curiosity burns inside me like the smoldering of punk wood. The island encourages these thoughts. It offers an open forum of friends to puzzle over mysteries.

This is where I bring Mckenzie and Kip. Home.

Chapter Two

Pulling Down the Sky

May in the Pacific Northwest can be anything. Our weather is wet and cold one day, then so bright the next that the sun makes the green grass cry out. I like the misty days, the days of creation. There is the story of how Coyote pulled the world up out of the mist. In the north, Coyote is Crow or Raven. Crow and Raven made a pact with Wolf. They would show her where the game is if she would share her kill.

On the island, my little round cabin sits in a tall stand of dark fir trees. Beyond this is a wide meadow carved from the forest. Great ferns grow beside the cabin and peek in the cabin's many windows. These giant ferns give the forest a primitive feel. I can always hear the wind, even the slightest rustle.

By trade I am a teacher and trainer of horses. It is a lifestyle rather than a job. My boots are always muddy, my hands are callused. And after twelve-hour days I am smelly. It is hard to have a social life. Very few men in my life have understood my total dedication to my work. My days are filled with horse personalities rather than people. I ponder why a colt would rather buck than jump. Colts are not broke but started, explained to. Horses talk like dancers and so I have learned to use the voices of the body. I speak with the touch of my hand, a flashing glance, or the way I hold myself on their backs. I had to learn that I am a horse. At least I have trained so long that the horses think I am. Because of the horses, I have learned to trust my body. I can put my consciousness in other parts of my body other than the part that wears my hat. So, if I am psychic, it comes from my heart, not from my head.

In time, the horses invaded my art. They gallop into my stone sculptures and line drawings and paintings on glass. With a point and chisel, I bang with my hammer, chasing stone with salt water. The white rock laughs—I make a self-portrait. The alabaster horse stares at me with eyes of stone, heart of glittering dust. My art becomes my children, along with my animal companions. I look at creation. My nephews are my family's life blood that flows down from the outstretched hands of the ancestors. But my children are time capsules of stone and paper and bright paint. My children have hard hooves and yellow eyes.

My first days on the island with the animal babies are awkward as I try to figure out where to put them. The slinking wolf cub trips loosely around me, stealing everything: the rug under my feet, my shoes, my hat. I try to save the floors of polished hardwood from damage, but it may be impossible. After about ten days Mckenzie surprises me when she begins to howl with Peter. A thin, high-pitched howl comes from Mckenzie as she raises her head to join Peter with his deep, melodic voice. I wonder if she is not more surprised than I am. Her sweet voice weaves into my heart and quickly, Mckenzie becomes my daughter. And slowly, slowly our life together begins to settle.

Outside on the wide porch I watch the wind pull long dark

clouds over my cabin. The trees twist in the motion of the sky. Mckenzie pulls at my boots as if telling me, *Let's go do something*. She is a good wolf, except for getting up so early to eat and crapping on everything. When I look at Mckenzie, she reminds me of a drum beat, a flute song.

I am as restless as the infant wolf, so I scoop up the eight weeks of fur, breathe her in, and walk toward a single old tree that stands in the meadow. The original family of trees was logged years ago, but not this one. It is not huge, or twisted with some remarkable design. Perhaps the loggers felt something and left it standing. We walk in this order: me, Peter, Beanie, Mckenzie, then Kip. The little fox is the most adventurous. He goes off on side tracks of his own, forcing me to stop and search for him. Mckenzie stays close watching my every move with military alertness. Of course, she is a social creature and Kip is not. I have seen foxes keep the same range and mate over several years. But they are usually more solitary than the wolves.

At the base of the tree I finger feathers torn from the breast of a pheasant killed by an eagle. The ground is damp and the smell of hay creeps out of the grasses. The feather is striped and there is a bit of dry dark blood clinging to the down. This feather was torn out as the eagle plucked its prey, holding it down with its great talons. Tracing my cheek with the feather's tip, my back rests solidly against the tree. My mind drifts into a plain, a land of grass where I wind thoughts around. Who makes the voices speak inside our heads? Does the land have an unconscious that comes into being by dreaming? By myth? Is this what speaks to us? When I close my eyes I see something, I hear something.

I thought I knew myself. I am a professional horse trainer who jumps solid fences at high speed. Horse and I throw ourselves over a fence and we become something wild. We run with instinct, every tooth bared. It is like madness, singeing the soul hot. I think that death can never touch me if we gallop, but death is well mounted too. The horse gives us this strength. I know what the running elk

feels. I can speak and listen with my body. But the tighter I hold on to my life, the more likely I am to lose it. But when I let go of it, then I survive. I keep my wilderness. The choke hold of fear, domestication, frightens me. The horse calls me back: *It is more honorable to fall then to stop.* When I first came to the island the horses warned me that I no longer believed or trusted the wild.

Mist clings to the top of the grass. Water is the beginning of the blood of the land. The island only has the water that falls on it, so does the world. The blood of North America runs through me. I stare at my hand, the veins push up blue-green against olive skin. Grandpa said Osage. Was that right? Mom said that she was proud of her Native blood; "But don't ever call me an Arkie." Why does this thought bolt into my mind like a young horse? Words keep floating, sparkling, in my head. Myth strings words like wool along the edges of my mind. Something old reaches in and pulls out long threads of ideas like an old woman who sits at her loom. The tree reaches up and pulls the sky down... Trees bridge the gap between the Sky Father and Earth Mother.

Kip at three months.

I am confused, I cannot see the pattern, but I write my first poem and trust.

I don't know...
I think the tree reaches up
and pulls the sky down—-
I can see that from my window.
"Grandfather?
Is that you pulling down the sky?"

Fox boy walked by my house yesterday
from the edge of the meadow,
from the circle of trees.
I think Fox knows something.
He winked...
He winked and then stuck his tongue out at me.
But maybe he was licking his whiskers.
"Grandfather,
Grandfather...
Ask that fox to tell me his secret.
His secret from the circle of trees."
Grandfather smiles and squints.
"Oh my Granddaughter,
you already know that one...!"

"Is it in my pockets,
my pockets Grandfather?
In my mackinaw?
In my jeans?"
Eagle Man saw me looking in my pockets,
in my jeans.
He screamed...
Eagle Man.

"No, no Granddaughter,
not in pockets.
Not that way,
the other way.
In your hands,
in your eyes,
from your spirit.
There's the secret,
right where Coyote left it."
Grandfather walked,
walked up the tree,
looked down, and let go of the sky.

The little wolf pokes her head up out of the grass and stares at me. The color of her eyes is starting to change. At first they were clear blue, now they are a muddy turquoise that will soon become golden. Mckenzie drags around oversize feet in a parody of the loose legged, graceful wolf trot. She sniffs the feathers. Kip has disappeared into the long grass. Kip and Mckenzie then follow

McKenzie at three months.

me on small but steady legs back to the cabin. I drop the feather and it goes to the ground like a quail to the brush. I write down more thoughts.

At first, Mckenzie lives in what passes as my bathroom. This is because of her muck. Wolves are almost, but not impossible, to house break. The trick is to have an adult wolf to imitate. Mckenzie has Peter. From the beginning, Peter has been totally in love with the small gray cub. He follows her around and offers her comfort at the right time. Beanie tolerates the wolf, but growls and snaps if she begs food from her. Mckenzie rears up on her hind legs and grabs at Beanie's mouth trying to lick inside it. This is a signal for a wolf mother to regurgitate her food. Beanie thinks it is disgusting. My friends call it wolf dental hygiene. Peter lets her beg from him, but strangely, rarely offers her food from his stomach. Perhaps it is because Peter is half dog. A part of him has forgotten the old ways.

In time, they all learn how to climb the stairs to the loft where they sleep with me. Mckenzie likes to sleep on top of my head, straddling her furry body across my forehead. Mckenzie is a pompous bedmate. Even from the beginning if I move too much she growls, then licks me to apologize. Kip has a little box that he sleeps in. When he was tiny the box was no problem. I put it by my mattress, and Kip rattled a bit, but he was content because he was close to his family. However, foxes grow quickly. Soon Kip makes Mckenzie look like an infant. Now, he hates his crate. I try to keep him confined at night because he spreads his dung around the house. However, when he is locked in his crate overnight he screams at the top of his voice. Kip wants to be in bed with us and prefers sleeping on my chest or near my feet. But Kip is nocturnal. So I gave up and most nights he wanders at will, prowling the house.

One night I woke up with a huge full moon peering through the uncurtained window. The light swam in and filled the cabin like a snowy stream. I glanced up and saw the form of Kip, his black coat outlined in silver. He came down out of a slow swinging arc from a high pounce, aiming for my eyes. That moment hung, suspended in front of me. His little pointy face was full of amusement and curiosity and a wild bacchanal joy. I caught him and ruffled his fur, then set him down and he scurried away. Babies must pounce and scuffle if they are to learn their trade. The tolerance of wild mothers must be great.

Kip

It is interesting how the future stalks us, hiding and waiting while we, like deer, come down to the water to drink. When Mckenzie first joined my life on the island, I still believed in time. But already my relationship to time is changing. Moments turn into hours. I live simply in my cabin without running water and electricity. I have a lot of time to think and observe nature's small gifts. In my busy life before moving to the island I never had time for moments to turn into hours. Instead, I was always in the future, thinking about what I had to do next. Now, with Mckenzie and Kip, time moves in a circle.

As I lie on the seat of my truck, resting, before I begin another

work day, I think about the horse business. Once, on a street in Alaska a drunk man walked up to me and said, "Yes, the horses are the only way for you now." Then he winked and staggered away. What are the odds of someone I don't know just walking up and saying that to me? Was it coincidence or is there a gathering of the unconscious that connects all of us? And had this man tapped it? An old Native man on a mountain heard me say once, "I have no people, really. No culture. The Native part is forgotten and Italy is far." He replied, "Your people will find you." I must trust the unconscious wind and sea that will bring them.

In the afternoon light, the owner of the horses walks up and as her shadow falls on me, I open my eyes. Her words reach out and grab me: "You look like an Indian." Something jumps up inside of me, but doesn't speak. My heart cannot feel these words for too long. I have to get to work jumping horses over solid fences. The horses don't care if I'm Indian, but perhaps they know.

Indian? What is that? I ask myself. *Italian? What is that?* The old man from my childhood looks at me from the red dust of memory on a blue mountain. He speaks, "As the blood of the land runs equal so does the blood of all life run equal.... Everything is one. We were all Native peoples once." This I believe. A Blackfeet friend told me about "wannabes." A "wannabe" is a non-Native who wants to be Indian. He said that those people aren't really "wannabes," they are "used-to-bes."

After work I return to the cabin and wander through the forest, the cedar needles pricking my bare feet. The thrush sings his music, and it drifts through the air circling the thick trees. Kip trots through my legs, one broad-furred paw grazing my foot. He sits down on the porch like a tiny cat and stares at me seriously. His expression asks, *Where is Mckenzie?*

After a quick look around the little wolf yard surrounded by chain-link fence, I call. No little baggy gray form comes trotting up with deep serious eyes. The sky is darkening. Gentle rain falls speaking in its soft voice, rinsing the dusty salal leaves. Where is she? I look around the cabin. I search the wolf pen again. Mckenzie is small enough for an eagle or owl to snatch. Peter and Beanie join me, concerned. Mckenzie is gone. What will I do if I never find her? What if she is lost and dies because she got out of a small hole in the pen? How can humans love another of a different species? *Oh Ho!* The old man in my memory laughs at that question. *There are no others!*

I call the neighbors and they come at once and help me look. We search through fern and barberry, and the thrush keeps singing. My neighbor Joe, the Vietnam veteran, searches with his two small children. He says, "I don't think she'll come back." I secretly name him, "Don't Joe." He wears black and his face is stretched by sorrow. Those who did not come home from the war affect him. He rescues wounded soldiers.

People have to go home. Still no Mckenzie. We search till the rain falls heavily and the darkness drops like a felled tree. I sit and feel the old familiar heaviness of my life story. My father, Pop, his cold hands waxy, filled with death instead of warm blood. I think of Granny, her eyes bright, like a jay-bird's, with drugs and hallucinations of fire. I remember my old horse, The Corinthian, as he turned and looked at me when the trailer came to take him away to retire. Loss of a loved one.

But today the universe sighs, *Not yet*. There is a soft rustling, a quiet noise stirring in the rain. A little gray head drowsy with sleep ambles out of the salal. Mckenzie had been only four feet from my front door. The little wolf taught me from the beginning that she was not a dog. The Gray One comes when she wishes.

That night the wolves howl in my dreams. I walk on snow-covered mountains with Mckenzie. She is full grown and strong. We are searching for something. A deer springs before us and we chase it. Mckenzie and I kill the deer and eat it. Looking down I notice my black paws.

I am a wolf when I sleep.

Chapter Three

Living with Coyote

The island roads curve gently around the dark water of Puget Sound. The wind is combed by the tall emerald fingers of the fir trees. Driving these roads, I reach up with one hand and gently remove Kip from the dashboard. He loves to ride in the car, his little black feet poised on the dash, long bushy tail flung out for balance, sniffing curiously at the dizzy sights that rush by faster than he can run.

Mckenzie lies between the front seats and lazily licks the stick shift. Glancing down, I push her nose away. "No!" I say firmly. Mckenzie is taste testing. She glares up at me, intelligence swimming in those intense eyes. I grasp the shift, all sticky with starchy wolf spit, and downshift into second gear.

Beanie sits in the passenger seat erect, seriously gazing out the windshield. Beanie, the captain, who has worked horses with me for eight years, chasing colts into my grasp. Every now and then Beanie glances disgustedly at the little fox and wolf as if she had never seen such uselessness.

Peter, the big gray, half-timber wolf, lies asleep in the back of the Jeep. His snoring provokes Kip to stare curiously at his muzzle, and pant his peculiar greeting. Peter, the emperor of this little world, pays no attention. If it had been a marauding bear or snake he would act his role. But the little fox is ignored.

Mckenzie starts to trot around inside the Jeep. Wolves are animals who travel great distances in the wild. She paces in the car as we drive and I fancy she sometimes imagines she is migrating across the tundra following the great columns of caribou in the bright days of an arctic summer. Mckenzie is learning to ride in the car for her own good as well as for mine. She is capable of sitting calmly while the car is motionless or for short excursions into town, but the longer journeys will be a challenge.

The wolves are very particular about their vehicle. They are contrary about getting in and out, and do so only as fancy inspires them. They will not ride in just any old car and they decide when they will go. It is almost impossible to lift an unwilling wolf. The psychological effect of their teeth is powerful. They lie down flat, limp, and relaxed, getting heavier. If I persist in picking up half of a wolf, either front or back, he growls, a reminder that *he* chooses. If that does not stop me, he snaps at my arm. The sound made by a wolf snapping is like a cartoon alligator's—a deep popping. A wolf's fangs are long, but snaps are generally pulled before contact with flesh is made. Fortunately, wolves are more into gesture than physical violence.

But if I continue, perhaps muttering, "Get up you lazy old dusty thing," The wolf grabs my arm in his teeth, snarling, as if to say, *Look, move me where I don't want to go, and we're going to have problems. Your problems will be bigger than mine.* He then looks at me with a frank arresting stare, the strength of mountains rumbling in his eyes. My rule with wolves: never force an issue. Bribery seldom works, even with their favorite treats. They know when I try to fool them and they act accordingly.

One of my other problems is that the wolves tend to eat the car. Slowly but surely I lose turn indicators, seat belts, seat. The

Beanie at seven years.

Peter at six years.

Kip at three months.

Mckenzie at three months.

final straw was the dashboard. Of course, this was before I had invented "Wolf Away" and had sprayed it throughout the car. The active ingredients in my homemade wolf repellent include whiskey, Tabasco, and tar. I had a difficult time explaining to a state trooper the reason why I could not signal and why I had no seat belts. The wolves were not in the car to verify my story when I was stopped, but the officer was intrigued by the Jeep's strange smell.

I do not know why I drive everywhere with the wolves. It may be a hereditary eccentricity. (Perhaps the same eccentricity that made my Grandpa Natali jump off the Brooklyn Bridge. At the time he was an inventor and was trying out a type of "Mae West" life-preserver.) I hate to leave the wolves at home. A friend asked me, "T? Why do you drive the wolves around?" I told her I was airing them. She took a sniff in the Jeep and said, "Yes, they seem to need airing."

One time the wolves actually saved me from physical harm. I was driving along, rather slowly, when suddenly a car passed me. It pulled in front of the Jeep, then stopped. I had to slam on my brakes, sending the agitated wolves flying forward. A man leaped out of the car ahead of me, and ran up to my window, and started screaming. He was an expert at cursing. Perhaps he thought I was someone else, but when he threatened me with physical violence, something dark rose up in my heart. The wolves sensed danger, and crowded together for support. Beanie barked furiously. Peter thrust his head towards the half-open window and from his throat came an extremely serious rumble, a grumbling groan from deep in his chest.

Mckenzie looked directly into the man's face. She locked eyes with him. Wolves do this to test the vulnerability of prey. She made no sound at all, but the fur on her back stood straight up. Her lips lifted, revealing the young but impressively long canines of a hunter. I rolled the window down a few more inches hoping

the man did not have a gun. With a low voice I said as smoothly as I could, "Do you want me to let them out?"

As if lifted up by strings, the man did an incredible about-face, jumped in his car, and sped away. For some strange reason, I could not resist taking off after him. Wolves will always chase what runs, so my decision was met with approval by the golden eyes behind me. We flew around turns, up hills, and roared down empty roads. I could see the man staring in his rearview mirror fixedly, as if he could not believe his eyes. The wolves pressed against the windshield, eyes blazing, tongues lolling, eager for the pursuit. I yelled a couple of whoops, which set the wolves to howling. The gathering of the pack. Speeding around the island this way for miles, my friends saw the procession. They turned questioning faces towards me, and hesitantly waved.

Jerkily, I managed to scribble down the man's license number. I realized that there was nothing else I could do. Finally, pity caught up to the anger caused by my fear and I let the man speed away. The wolves were disappointed that this guy, potential prey, was so healthy. When they hunt, wolves chase the infirm. That man could drive fast. He was obviously in great shape!

I drove to the little courthouse to report the incident. Because it was Tuesday there was a police officer on duty. He was in a small room with a cup of coffee. His head in his hands, he seemed to be holding a severe headache. Larry the fisherman and Linda the school bus driver had told me that the local police come from the toughest beats. They come to rest on the little rural island.

The officer listened wearily to my story and then got up and took a look at the Jeep from the window. Kip was sitting on the dash. He looked at the fox and said, "Lady, that is a strange cat!" He then sat down and quietly put his head back in his hands. I gave him the license number. He said sadly, "We'll check it out."

The local librarians, Jan and Rayna, ask if I would give a lecture on wolves at the library. Jan, a tall slender woman with an amazing shock of wild curly Scottish hair, is in love with wolves. This is something I see a lot of. The wolf is a symbol that hunts deep in the human spirit. I agree to speak knowing that if Mckenzie destroys the library she will be forgiven by Jan.

Mckenzie at three months.

The night of the lecture comes, and the darkness brings out the rich scents of the land and sea, sweet cedar and salty beach stones first rolled round by the surf. The moon, like a wolf mother, peers between the clouds at the sleeping nest of the world. Fortunately, the wolves decide it is a traveling kind of night, and they easily get in the Jeep.

The library's meeting room is packed when I arrive. About eighty people are squeezed into a room designed for fifty so I leave the wolves in the car while I talk. The gathering is willing to hear about what is happening in Alaska. The state government still allows the killing of wolves, even though the wolf is on the country's endangered species list. The wolf keeps the game animals strong by hunting and by killing the weak and the sick.

And perhaps more important, the wolf has a right to live.

Some people believe that by watching the wolf the first humans learned about hunting and caring for their family. Why is the wolf a symbol of the perfect hunter and loving parent to some, and to others the wolf is a vicious killer who hunts lambs and children? Is it because we feel guilty about killing for food and the wolf is the scapegoat? There was a time long ago when all people admired the wolf. That was the time when we, too, were wild. The wolves live in a way that humanity longs for. I see this in the round wide eyes that face me during the lecture.

Silently, I wonder, *Why do people want wolves as pets?* Perhaps it is the loss of our own wildness. And the soul, trapped in suburbia, mirrors the capture by taking a wild animal as a prisoner. How do I tell these people that wilderness slips through fingers like water? Cup the hand, lift it to your mouth, and drink the sweet water from the land. That is how the wild is held within. A scientist once told me that she prefers not to use the term, "return to the wild," when talking about the reintroduction of wild animals to their natural habitat. I asked her what would she call it. She replied, "Free ranging." Holding back rising anger, I responded, "Like chickens?"

Why do we fear wildness? Is it because it takes away our dominion over all? Will it place us back in the dirt next to the campfire, while around us in the darkness the panther walks and wolves howl? If there is no wildness, what will be the nature of the land? Are we afraid we will become like the domestic cow and sheep with nothing to sharpen our wits against? Yes, I think there should be some domesticity, but in balance with wildness. People have said to me, "Well, you can die in the wild. And those beasts you admire are killers." The mirror is sometimes frightening. Of course I can be killed. I must die of something and I prefer a few seconds of terror to a slow death of spirit.

At the end of the talk, Mckenzie comes into the library. A dancer on big silent paws, her eyes stare intently as if ready to

stalk whatever moves. But she is nervous and I can not bring her directly into the crowd. The room is quiet, like a herd of deer listening for panting breath.

Behind the glass doors that divide the main library room, the people stand quietly in the hallway. Outside, they peep in at a wolf among the books. Mckenzie is well behaved that night except for jumping up on the main counter and leaving a large pile of dung to mark her territory. The children are very impressed. In the future, every time I go to the library and lay my books on the counter, I know I will remember the dung, and all the humans, like wild animals with staring eyes.

The world speaks to us in many ways, but how? And what does she say? Does she talk of robes and ritual? Or is her speech as simple and clear as a child's wish to play in the bright water of a creek, hands dabbling, feeling the coolness, the wetness. The breeze blows the trees and thoughts come. I listen and another poem rises.

I dreamed one night,
I dreamed I stood on a wide meadow
full of grass, blue flowers,
rock, insects.
Birds flew, the air moved,
the sky turned.

"What was that?"
Tortoise Old Man looked out.
"Nothing, daughter."
"No, I felt it. I saw it."
Tortoise smiled slow.
"Oh that.
That was your mother breathing."

Living with Coyote

At the ranch where I worked before I moved to the little island I often rode a big stallion along the dry roads of Northern California's ranch country. His hard hooves made muffled noises in the soft dirt. One special afternoon I saw a red-tailed hawk, wings flapping, slowly land a few yards away. It was as if we were alone in the world. She was dark, her tail the color of blood. The hawk watched, turned her head one way then another, and suddenly pushed off with a simple thrust. One of her tail feathers dropped like a prayer. I jumped off the bay and ran to pick up the feather, still warm at the quill end. Above, the hawk screamed *Ki hiiiiii*, and looked down.

A week after my meeting with the hawk, one of the ranch hands told me that there was a bull buffalo on the grass in front of my house. He had gotten loose from the neighboring ranch. Astonished, I ran to see. The buffalo was as big as a boulder with smoky eyes and hooves as bright as obsidian. I walked up to the buffalo with a bucket of grain and he followed me into a paddock.

The hawk and the buffalo called to my Native blood. I worried about my own freedom, thought of the open plains. Life seemed too complicated, too hurried, even in the horse business. Sharing these feelings with a jockey friend, he showed surprise and said, "What are you going to do, move into the mountains and grow vegetables?" "No, I'm not sure what I'll do. But running horses for other people, so busy with no time to think, that's not working for me." My friend insisted, "You'll always do horses, T. You're the kind of person that has them in your blood. You'll be back." "Maybe, but not the same."

The signs that the world brought me—-the hawk and the buffalo—-woke some sleeping part of myself. In the hills of

Northern California behind my house the coyotes howled. Soon after those events, the buffalo's tracks still visible in front of my house, I gave my notice and moved.

Here on the island I still work with the horses, but it's changing. A friend tells me, "My god, Teresa, you are almost forty, you shouldn't be starting colts any more." "Oh," I say, "should I die in a rest home?"

You eat life or life eats you.

The wild knows that when you are still be still. But when you hunt or graze or love do not hesitate. Watch, be cautious, but realize hesitation can kill you. Ah, that is the strange part. Action can kill you too. But in action there is education. We learn by making mistakes, not by being perfect.

I admire horses and wolves for their family loyalty. Both pairs bond into a group. Can a husband or wife make up the entire village? They cannot. Horses and wolves are practical. They know the season of love and understand the beauty of friendship. Not all intimate friendships are physical. But for some reason popular culture makes it seem that the general public copulates every chance it gets.

Some of my friends are afraid of love tangles and pain. Where is the partnership that wildness pushes upon the individual? Oh, I'm at fault too. Men have said, "Gee, Teresa, be softer." Then they scrape a thoughtful granite hand across their jaws and their eyes squint up. A friend and I loved each other one afternoon after I said, "Why haven't we?" Later, when he was swimming with the buffalo bull men, they asked, "What is that mark?" My friend smiled and said he had laid down with Wolf Woman. But wolves are not promiscuous.

One night Coyote showed up in my dreams to explain the sexes. When I woke I wrote the dream down. I had heard it somewhere before. Had one of the old people told it to me and I just remembered it? This is what Coyote told me:

Living with Coyote

"What do you mean
Man and Woman
are the two sexes?"
Said Coyote to
me one night.
"You know," I answered.
Coyote shook himself
"Well, you're wrong
on that one."

Grandfather in the
corner started giggling.
"Oh well, then
how many sexes are there?"
Coyote yawned and said, "For people, eight."
"Eight?" I asked.
"How can there be eight?"
Coyote recited
as Grandfather counted
off on his fingers.
"Woman who loves man.
Man who loves woman.
Woman who loves woman.
Man who loves man.
Man loving as woman.
Woman loving as man.
The one who is both.
The one who is alone.
Got that?"
said Coyote and he
curled up to go to sleep.

Perhaps I prefer the one who is alone. Someone asked me what it meant for me to be a woman. I said I am a human being first, then I think of my ancestry and the wolves and horses. And after that, I think of being a woman. I am a human being. My eyes are Mediterranean. My heart is Osage. I am a woman.

There is great honor having a woman's body and spirit. No wonder there came a time when men feared this power. Oh, the power swings one way then another, eventually to stabilize somewhere in between. A man, long ago, was bloodied in war. A woman bleeds every month. Her life is proof of continuation.

The women are there,
the women are there,
walking up the narrow trail,
with blood stained hands,
holding the baby to the Eastern Light.

The women are there,
the women are there,
watching the child play in the Green Land.
The women are there,
the women are there,
in the darkness,
wrapping the dead in Elk Person's skin.

The women are there.
Men People don't forget this,
the women are there!

I see my Great Grandmother sitting in the snow,
long white braids,
Smiling,
shaking the rattle, saying,
"The women are there,
the women are there."

Chapter Four

Sister Wolf

My Grandpa's hair has only the beginnings of white through a river of black. His face has thick lines that slide like otters next to his bowed nose. A determined, sometimes bitter expression surrounds dark eyes that flash stubborn resentment, stopping questions in their tracks. Grandpa Albert is tough, maybe bitter, from more than eighty years of life's hard offerings. His mother had died in his arms of TB when he was twelve years old. And when she died, the stories of the Osage ancestors were silenced.

Grandpa spoke little to my mother about the Native ways, unlike my Italian father, who was an expert in extreme emotion; soaringly happy or miserable like an ancient hero. Pop talked about his family, how they had emigrated to America from Italy in the early part of the century. In the beginning Pop told me that his mother was from Naples and his father from Rome. Later he confided that his mother and father were from a southern city in Calabria and the Sicilian city, Palermo. In Italy there are prejudices against the darker people from the south. The prejudices are as old as the shore people, the first people of the Mediterranean.

Pop's stories were also about life in Brooklyn, poor and near starving, and their move to Long Island where they could hunt and fish. Grandpa Natali worked on inventions and Grandma Connie rebuked the Mob in Italy for the terror they had inflicted on her family in Brooklyn. Pop also talked about his family of nine children. Five died before they were two years old, and two died as a result of World War II. This left only Pop and Uncle Bob.

But Grandpa Albert told us very little about his family. We know that we have a Scots-Irish ancestor who came to the United States in the 1700s. We also know we are Native. I could not remember much else. But I was struck by the connection that my ancestors in Italy, tenant farmers, had been kicked off their land and came to the United States; and my ancestors, the Osage, were kicked off their land by the United States government.

Today there is a need to return to tribalism, to identify with a particular group of people. I have heard it spoken of as a negative thing, as something that does not promote unity. But the world is already one. The body has many parts. My feeling of emptiness, of looking for my ancestors is really my looking for the earth. It is a need to feel that I belong to the land as much as the cedar or elk. Many times I have wondered, *Why have we separated ourselves?*

Mckenzie plays and tumbles across the porch as intently as the questions and memories in my mind. The wolf cub grows so rapidly that at nearly four months she is almost the size of Beanie who weighs about sixty pounds at six years old. McKenzie is perfectly at home in her body like a dancer with a trusted script and choreography. Her soul fills her the way wind fills the sails of a ship

Sitting, quietly watching her, a thrush flies by, framing the morning with his songs. Mckenzie's eyes lock on the bird who lands on the dark-green salal bush inside the wolf pen. The branch swings under the bird's slight weight. Wolf eyes follow the bird, drawn by its vibrating life. Slowly, exquisitely, Mckenzie crouches and begins to stalk. The sight of a young animal creeping with such seriousness makes my skin prickle. Her eyes never waver, her body

is filled with innocent grace and the knowledge of death. I already see her calm acceptance of taking a life. But today, the bird lives, the wolf lives, they both in turn will give back in their own time. Overhead a hawk screams and the thrush flies off, the moment broken. Mckenzie prances gaily up to where the bird has been, her eyes joyful.

Face to the sky, I watch the hawk spiral in the sacred gyro. Somewhere inside me, I know there are ancestors listening. They stand up to watch the hawk, remember the Plains and the hunting of wolves. I begin thinking of the Native nations. Finally, I call Grandpa. Our conversations are stiff.

"What People are we Grandpa?"

"What?"

"What tribe are we?"

"Osage, I think."

"You're not sure?"

"Look, Teresa Ann, my father and mother never talked about it. It's foolishness bringing it up now." That is all he would say.

Kip, Peter, Beanie, Mckenzie, and I walk in the meadow. I touch the boulders that the glaciers dropped. Cool, smooth stone, alive, slowed down, graceful. The boulders stand, polished by ice. Where is my place? What forces would polish me as smooth as the rivers of ice? Finding a dead falcon, I remove the two sharp primary feathers, alternately striped dark and light. I bury the little bird, covering its fierce eyes with the soft mossy dirt, a final nest by the fir tree. I leave a few of my hairs in return for the feathers.

I have few neighbors. One is a man who is keenly interested in Native ways although his ancestors are from Europe. Talking with him is a paradox. He tells me things that I already know. But there seems to be imbalance. Why choose a belief system not of your own blood? Is it because he lives on this land? But he follows Plains tradition, which is different from the cultures of the Pacific

Northwest. Is it because his own European people had forgotten the traditions of the earth that have now almost disappeared into the dust? Something is missing from him that he desperately needs. In my own heart the same is missing. But deep inside I hear a flute song, drumming, and the howling of wolves.

Mckenzie and Kip are starting to be real troublemakers. Both work on the cabin with their sharp little teeth. Wolves use their teeth like fingers, feeling and exploring. Mckenzie rips things apart then cheerfully discards them. It is tough in the early morning to be startled out of bed by Mckenzie's chewing. Kip is impossible to housebreak. His long manure falls in the

most bizarre places. The faucet and the rim of a coffee mug seem to be favorites. When I stumble out of the loft to make a fire and brew coffee, I am confronted by the strangely decorated mug.

Beanie flushes a rat from the corners and leads Mckenzie on a jerky twisting chase through my cabin. The dog grabs the fleeing rat who turns in Beanie's mouth fighting to survive. Beanie kills the rodent then drops it at Mckenzie's gray feet. The young wolf looks at it curiously, then glaring in my face, she ferociously eats it. I watch in amazement. Already I can see we share a life together and that Mckenzie thinks that whatever is mine is

hers. She is not a pet. We are becoming more like sisters as she gets older.

Those misty mornings, like sunlight shot through pearl, I write down phrases that get caught in my mind the way clouds cling to mountains. Then the thoughts come like rain. When I reread them I feel old. Not old in a bad way, tottering and grumpy, but old with the energy of ancient things like the sea, the stars. The words comfort me and bring back memories and events from my past. Again, they take on flesh and walk before me and make sense.

For the Osage

Call me up Stars,
Call me up Stars,
you Star People,
call me
call me up.

But slowly,
slowly,
call up my spirit first,
Star Ones.
Call up my mind next, Stars,
call up my body last
and I'll dance with you,
dance the white road way.

You Star People,
call me up.

I show my writing to a neighbor who asks me if I am Native. I pause and answer, "Partly." That inspires me to call Grandpa again. I remember a family dinner from almost a lifetime ago. Grandpa talked to Pop about the people coming from the sky and the Native way he walked, sometimes stepping on the earth with the front of his foot first. When I asked Grandpa about that memory, he only would say, "I don't remember it." I wonder if I had dreamed it.

Numerous times I call Grandpa. And for a long time I get the same answers. Then one evening lit faintly by the sun quickly vanishing behind a curtain of forest, Grandpa softly told me this: "My mother said we could go and live on the reservation." "What?" My breath hissed back. "It was so long ago, Teresa Ann. Mother said that she didn't want to go there and get mixed up in all of that. It was too far and dangerous." That was all Grandpa would say that night. After our conversation thoughts pile onto one another like horses herded through a narrow draw. They did not go to the reservation? Why? Ashamed? Proud?

For months I can only guess and stare at a cold tin-type photograph. One face draws me in again and again. Great-Grandmother Nettie, a dark woman in an old-fashioned dress. The dress is tame, restricting, awkward. Her face, beautiful, mysterious, wild. She calls to me. Her voice echoes through the tin-type and falls into Mckenzie's throat. My relatives on that side of the family are silent, except through the wolves.

I wonder about the Osage. What would the people on the Osage reservation say to me? Their families stayed when mine moved on. Grandpa finally explained to me that his family decided to stay in Arkansas. They did not want the reservation. They did not get involved with the oil money when it was discovered on Indian land. They did not seek tribe enrollment when asked to travel back to Oklahoma to register with the government at the Osage reservation.

My Italian half is used to the comradeship that Italians give one

another. The old Italian question is, *What part of Italy are you from?* When I call the Osage reservation the woman asks, *What clan are you from?* She has heard a story like mine many times. She puts me on hold to answer another call. Soon another woman comes on the phone and asks in a gruff voice, "Who is this?" I tell her my name. "Well, what do you want?"

I tell her about my grandpa, about my sadness, about losing my family stories and connection. I could not reclaim my Osage blood.

Great-Grandmother Nettie.

The woman listens patiently then her gruffness softly drops and she says, "Who told you to be ashamed to look for your people? Don't let anyone take away your blood. Would you ask African Americans how much blood they have? You may not find them ever, really. But you'll find your path, and you'll be able to look on either side." The Osage Nation sends me the book of their language so I can learn it. When it arrives, I find that the old people called the life force *Wah Kon Tah*, "The Mystery." The old people were humble. They acknowledged that they did not know everything, and called God "The Mystery."

A chance phone call between a writer friend and her friend, Curly, leads me further down the path toward my Native blood. She told Curly about me. A short time later I received a strange package in the mail, bent and folded. When I opened it, there was a single soft eagle plume, a four-direction crystal, some old stone scrapers, and a polished buffalo stone. They are gifts from Curly who becomes my friend. He invited me to the Blackfeet reservation to stay with his cousins, Darrell and Bob Blackbull.

Like thirst and hunger, the Plains call to me and I answer. With my wolves and dog I journey toward the Blackfeet reservation. After three days of driving, the Plains spread before me like a blanket of tall emerald. An incidental road broken with frost heave and no lines to divide it, rolls like a loose ribbon through the prairie. Grass waves twirl and dance. A swift sunrise, crimson and yellow like a meadow lark's throat, welcomes me. Standing in the grass with my hand at my waist, just touching the soft grass tips, tender with spring, my eyes are wet and bright. They sting at seeing the Plains for the first time. Curly's buffalo stone is in my hand, smooth and polished by the stomach acid of *pte*, Osage for buffalo.

The Blackfeet reservation is at the foot of the Rockies, which pour their water in four directions. The grass plains sweep in front of them. Here are the sunrises and sunsets, here is the land of the circling horizon.

Bob Blackbull is a cheerful man, who wears his hair pulled back in a braid. He is an idealist and romantic who dreams of the horses the ancestors rode. Darrell is more serious, more thoughtfully bent. His house is full of gifts the Native artists bring him. A mountain lion skin is draped over his old rocking chair. We have elk for dinner that night. While sitting in the house we stare out over the prairie to the lake where the trumpeter swans rest. We swap stories and I tell them of the Gray One. The men nod gravely and then smile.

The Plains of the Blackfeet Nation.

The next morning is clear and sweet. People come and go, sipping coffee, working to get ready for some art show or another. Silently, I watch Bob make jewelry. He looks up suddenly and catches my eye as he asks, "T, are you Native?" I had not told them, simply because it seemed strange. I look at him and answer, "Yes." "What nation?" Bob asks. "Osage." "Hummm, you look it," observes Bob, then he turns back to his work.

The wolves are with me, along with my dog Beanie. The elders watch me carefully and ask questions about where my blood comes from and what my clan is. My answers are in my Jeep panting to be let out to run. One man asks if I was raised traditional. I say no and tell them of my rural childhood and my Italian father. Bob laughs and fingers my pony bead necklace. "You know who made these beads?" he asks. "No." "Italians! You know what we call Italians, T?" "No." Bob starts chuckling, "Wopaho!" These folks are great kidders. Then Curly looks at me seriously and asks, "Where do you get your blood?" I tell him from my mother. He nods and sits down, content.

Looking at the wolves, another man says, "If you shoot a wolf your rifle will always shoot crooked after that." The wolves are sacred. Then he looks at me and asks, "You ever go down south?" "No." "Better not with those wolves," he warns. "Why?" I ask, simply. "They'll think you're a skin walker." "A what?" "A witch," the man replies, then turns away.

Later that day I decide to leave the busyness and drive out on the Plains, off the res to see what it is like. When I tell Bob my plans, he looks at me and says, "Be careful." His face is serious.

The gas station rests in a grove of trees. Cool cottonwood leaves dance sideways as I get out of the Jeep. I put gas in the car and walk to the little deli attached to the gas station. Stopping half way to tie my old tennis shoe, my long dark braid drags in the dust. I stand up and brush off my T-shirt, which reads, Native American Film Festival.

Inside the deli I pay for the gas, then get in line to order a sandwich. Two teenage boys sip slurpees as they stare at me and laugh quietly. I look down and around, not understanding the humor, oblivious to my Indian looks. The line moves forward and there is one guy in front of me and a woman behind me. I am next. I decide on a cheese sandwich, hungry because I had not eaten since morning. It is now late afternoon, and as I wait patiently, Bob's words ring in my ears. He had told me to be careful. Careful of what?

The man in front moves on with his sandwich in his hand. The woman behind the counter turns her eyes to the woman in back of me who immediately begins ordering. I wait till she is done then state, "I was next." The woman behind the counter never looks at me—-to her I do not exist. The other woman never acknowledges my presence, and waits patiently, looking past me, waiting for her order. The two teenage boys laugh out loud. Suddenly, I am cold.

I could be anything. My face is Mediterranean, my skin dark from sun is olive-russet, my eyes amber dark, my hair soft dusty black. I could be Greek, Italian, Iranian. But I had come off the res. My hair is braided and I am wearing beaded earrings that peek out from my hair. Far from home. Native at last. Now, it will never be

the same for me. I grew up near the Northern California coast. My friends were as varied as flowers, African, Mexican, Japanese. I remember a black girlfriend saying how sensitive she had become when she was exposed to this racial fear. She told me, "You always feel the arrows of eyes on you." Now I know this feeling. God, it must run deep and it must be taught.

My father had russet skin and blue-black hair, curly as a lambs. Once, as a child, I heard him say to a friend who was also Italian, "You know why we are like this? Our people married into North Africa. We are part of those people too." Who now will judge my search? We are all related. My soul reaches down into the earth and I hold my ancestors' flint. I look towards the azure Mediterranean

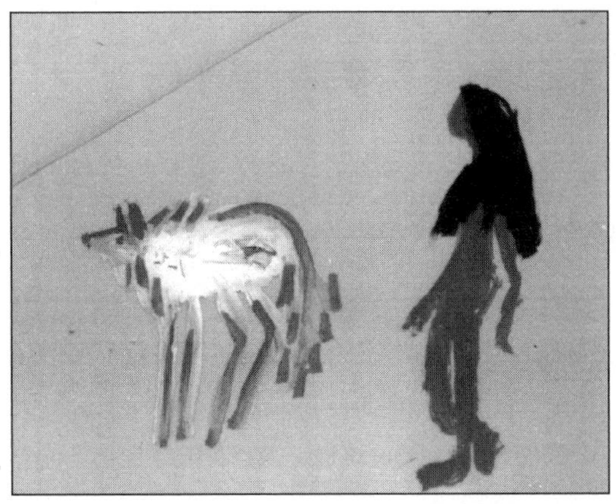

and the cold seas of Ireland and I know how cheetahs hunt because I am sure some ebony ancestor hunted with them. I *know* what I am. I am a human being. Wolves and horses do not care what color you are. And tundras wolves mingle with timber wolves as the snow plains run to deep forest.

I left the gas station, still hungry, and went back to the res. When I tell Bob about the incident, he says, "I told you, I told you." Then he adds his own story. "A couple of years ago I was almost killed in Billings. I was being beat up by some cowboys but some Crow guys came by and saved me."

That night I call Grandpa. I haltingly tell him what had happened. The old man is put out and angry. He says sternly, "Now you know why we didn't talk about it! Now, finally you know!"

In the north you tie out the dog. When they hear the wolf's howl the dogs bark and shiver, both in fear and longing to return to the pack. If the wolf comes close, two things can happen: A playful bow and a quick wag of the tail that means, *Come! Join us!* Or the soft stalking walk of hunger in glaring yellow eyes.

But wildness is a hard walk. It is a walk up mountains that makes you hungry and thirsty. There are stones that cut your knees and you fall. There are lions that are real with claws. And they can kill you with little effort. But the air is clean and cool and you can see a long way from those peaks into Tomorrow and back to Yesterday. And Now sits like a butterfly on your outstretched hand.

Come, Sister! the wolves howl, *put away your fear and run with us for a while.* Join the rainbow and live before you die. You must die of something. Live outside the cage. Then you won't become like a captive naked ape, interested only in sex and violence. You are a wild creature pure like wolves, beautiful like horses.

Chapter Five

Dreams of Wolves

One morning when I awake something lies quietly in my mind like a fawn in deep brush. Mckenzie stares at me intently. Her eyes are almost fully golden at four months. I glance at the young wolf and in my mind my great grandmother stares at me from the old tin-type photo, her wild, dark face above the tight and proper dress. A metallic taste sits in my mouth. Mckenzie, a captive wolf, looks through the chain-link fence at the world beyond my door. And the slender woman standing in front of the camera was told, "You must be civilized."

I slip back to my past and see myself at a United States Equestrian Team benefit. I am nineteen years old, a graduate of a program for a preliminary instructor certificate from the British Horse Society. I am also an Olympic team hopeful. My dress is black and long. My wild hair tightly braided, hangs at the back of my neck like a knife. People there speak of money and title. A British captain jumps on my stallion and winks at the blond woman who lowers her head meekly. But with the unblinking eyes of a hawk, I stare. There are cages, higher than we can jump, and we are taming ourselves out of the great gift.

Exactly how or when the idea for Mckenzie's release comes to me is difficult to pinpoint. Thoughts spin like wind in my head. All the tricksters of Native American beliefs, the bringers of fire, call out—I hear the voices of Coyote, Fox, Rabbit, Crow, and Raven. Suddenly the idea for Mckenzie's freedom hatches like the falcon chick on the edge of the cliffs.

I remember the rescued hawks who looked at the sky while we splinted their wings. The scrub jay and the dove—baby birds that I rescued and released as a child. Pop had shot a squirrel to eat. He cried over her in the sink, wiping his amber eyes on the dishtowel. He swallowed his tears when he saw me come in.

Granny and Mother fished and grew food for us as children. Now our bodies hear the wild trout swish through deep water in our minds, and the salmon swim in our blood. Deer swing their wary heads around to watch out of our eyes and the quail rustle behind our ears and call softly. Wild berries sweeten our words. Corn and beans and yellow crook-necked squash talk to us of the ancestors. Pop fed us wild meat.

The fawn rises from the underbrush of my mind—exposed. *Mckenzie must go back*. This I know. She must be taught to hunt, to find other wolves. She must be able to walk the forest path and go where she wishes, to birth cubs in the den she digs. If Mckenzie goes back, there is some part of me that will remain wild too. The blood will sing sweetly in my body. And Great-grandmother will smile. Perhaps the world is one, perhaps by saving the wilderness we are saving that part of the body that needs the lion's claws and the wolf's howl.

Mckenzie must go back, but how? I go through my workday riding horses. In the evening I rock in Great-grandmother's chair and watch fall start to rustle the leaves. Mckenzie comes to

me and sleeps the twitching restless napping of a wolf. The sea rolls in my mind.

The week turns around us. The sun keeps time and the moon measures the departing season. The idea grows feathers like the young falcon who stands facing the wind beating its wings, exercising to be strong enough to hold the air between sharp feathers.

First, the wolf must be isolated from people. Mckenzie must only be fed wild meat like that her parents would have brought her. I must take her to the wilderness so she can see for herself the scents and sounds. Mckenzie must test her strength as a hunter and test those who will be her prey in the give-away.

How can I do it? Perhaps it should not be me. In my hesitation, I call a rescue facility and in a halting voice give away my secret. "I have a wolf that I would like to give the chance to return to the wild." A woman's voice with a soft mother tone responds: "I understand. Is she purebred?" "Yes, she has a zoo pedigree." (Mckenzie's grandparents had been captured in the wild in the 1970s for a zoo, so she is pure wolf.)

"We would be happy to try to educate her and release her, but you understand she may die soon after the release." "Yes, I know." I glance at the wolf who is looking out the window, her eyes deep and clear. "Do you think it's the right thing to do?" I ask the woman. "Yes I do. This has been our job for years now, releasing wild animals that have been hurt. This will be a first for us because she was born in captivity, but I think she'll have a good chance if she is shy and predatory."

The woman explains their release technique, which is similar to my idea. We decide that they will come and pick her up tomorrow. I hang up the phone and the pain comes quickly, the re-twisting of the javelin. I cancel my horse lessons for the day, preferring to stay home and play with Mckenzie. Tonight we will be together for the last time.

The gray wolf nests on my chest. When she leaves where will my heart go? With her? Mckenzie does not notice my sorrow. She gnaws my hands, jumps at Peter who raises his head and stalks around proudly with Mckenzie hanging on to his ruff. Mckenzie and Kip grab a rug and tug at it playfully. Mckenzie could have easily eaten Kip, but she didn't—she thinks he is a relative.

In my mind, I see the little wolf in the mountains, running away from the crate in which the rescue facility had transported her. In her mind, will there be an empty place? Will Mckenzie look for me? Will she carry me in her heart? Will she hunt the deer thinking of the food I brought her? Will she steal down close to look at some hiker, and wonder?

Photo: Beth Biggs

Night comes and we lie down to sleep. Mckenzie curls up next to me. For much of the night I lie awake and listen to her breathing. I try to imagine what it will be like not to see her. Sleepless most of the night, I stare at the stars through the window. They glitter far away, seen through tears. The Osage came from the stars.

The sun looks down on grief and joy, apathy and excitement. Through the long lifetime of this star, it has shone whether or not the land was obscured by clouds. The morning is warm and the tops of the fir trees seem close and shining. Getting up and prodding my sleepy fire, the wolves follow me. Now, they follow the sadness in my body and sensing this, stand close. It is strange that the modern world has said that the animals, trees, plants, and stones feel nothing like

we do. I have heard that is the way to program someone for war. Tell soldiers that the enemy does not feel as they do. Then it is permissible to kill.

Camp coffee slowly brews in a pan. But the warm drink does not fill the emptiness inside. The phone stretches the moment harshly and I pick it up. It is the rescue center. "Teresa?" "Yes, is this Ruth?" "Yes. We have a problem." "What is it?" "I called my superiors about your animal and the Department of Wildlife and Fish and Game. They told us if we attempted this release that we would lose our license." Silence. The coffee boils away on the wood stove, the aromatic steam clouds the window. "Why?" is all I can ask. "Look, I'm not going to go into great detail. Or try to sort out right and wrong. You are dealing with a government bureaucracy. The wolf is on the endangered species list in the lower forty-eight states and it is a felony to own an endangered animal. Also, it is illegal to release the wolf and I can't risk the entire facility."

"I understand your point," I say, "but what am I going to do? I'm convinced that this is the right thing." The woman pauses, and takes a breath, "I think you should do it yourself." My sleeping dream from months ago comes back to me, chasing the morning away. In my dream I walked in snow-covered mountains with Mckenzie beside me.

Ruth keeps talking. "Look, you really already know the technique. Just do it like we were going to. You actually will have a better chance. I know in my heart that this is right." I turn and look at the three of them watching me—-the dog, the half wolf, and the wolf cub. Great-grandma Nettie's face in the tin-type photo stares, too. "I'll try." "Good luck Teresa, if any one asks you about what I said please forget it." "I will." Softly, Ruth offers a final "Good-bye."

I hang up the phone. Peter walks to the door and lifts one great gray paw to be let out. Mckenzie must go back. Now, I

must go back, remember my teachings, find my truths. The journey will be a hard one.

The forests of the Northwest are of two kinds. There is the great coastal rain forest with ancient dripping trees covered in blankets of moss. Among those trees I feel like a child. Those old woods are disappearing, and there are no wolves left in the rain forests of the coast. To the north are the Cascades that hold a stillness that eludes the woods of the Peninsula. These northern mountains are close to Canada, and small packs of wolves live in these thick, quiet forests.

I take McKenzie to two places in the beginning, both national parks in the Pacific Northwest. We try to go every other weekend. Few of my friends know of these secretive trips into the forests. The little wolf is timid at first, sticking close to my side on the narrow winding deer tracks through the twilight places. Peter is skilled in the woods and encourages the young wolf. Alone at night, far away in the mountains, I sit and think and watch and howl. That is how it is. In the woods, life rolls through me and I carry it back to my cabin. Those moments stay inside me like thunder's vibration that lasts long after the sound is gone. This is joy to me.

In the far northern woods I find wolf signs: tracks and scat in a meadow by a lake. The note paper of the wild. I place my palm in the track while Mckenzie excitedly runs up and down. The track is as big as my hand. I carry paper and pencil with me and add to the poems that I have written at the cabin.

I reread my earlier poems and understand that there is a part of myself that is hidden away, far from work and the expectations of this society.

Dreams of Wolves

In the morning
I walked with the wolves.
We go and see everyone.
As I walked over the grass,
my feet in their soft shoes,
the wolves with their big silent paws.
I heard many small voices
call out from where I was walking.

"Walk softly, sister," they said.
"There are many lives that are on your trail."

Years before on the ranch, I noticed that I began looking down when I walked, not seeing the beauty of the trees and hill-sides where I lived. Something was wrong. But now, walking the deer trails with Mckenzie, life becomes slower and richer, and I can breathe again. Sleeping outside brings back my childhood trust that the world will take care of herself and me as well. I wake and look at the stars or rapidly moving clouds, listen to the trees rustle and the small sounds of the woods. Mckenzie sometimes lies beside me or maybe she is off on one of her private adventures. If I awake without Mckenzie's presence I softly howl for her and then thrill when the silence is pierced by her musical answer. How lucky I am to have her call back to me! Her sweet voice raising in the dark like the land voicing her heart through the young wolf. Mckenzie and I are part of the land and accepted. We are at peace in the wild.

These are my days of dreams. I learn again how to be still and watch what is around me. The world rewards my patience. The mountains unfold like a piece of origami and the depth of creation is evident in the leaves, the creeks, the animals. I am held between the sky and earth. I am comfortable in the palm of the world: the business of ants coming and going to their bur-

row, the whistling cry of the hawk. Mckenzie and I walk gently through the land and the breeze. The deer guide us. My body becomes light and relaxes in these woods. At night I dream of wolves in the lap of the wild.

One day I have to doctor Mckenzie for a cut on her paw. She will not hold still, so I put a tranquilizer pill in the meat hoping that if she's sedated I can clean the wound. But she won't touch it. She knows when something has drugs in it. She only looks at me knowingly. So I have to risk letting her bite me. More than once I tell her, "Okay, if you wish to bite me

Photo: Beth Biggs

you'll just have to." She snarls when I start working and grabs my arm. Those teeth that can now crack the hardest leg bone for sweet marrow hold my arm softly. But I keep working, not daring to look. The old woman at the rescue center told me she almost had her arm amputated that way.

At five months old Mckenzie gave me my most noticeable wolf scar. I had given her a freshly caught rabbit and sat about twenty feet away to watch. She saw me stare, and in a fit of territorial jealousy, ran over and grabbed both of my hands in her

mouth. With her back teeth, sharp enough for shearing meat, she cut into my right hand leaving an inch-and-a-half gash. I held still, painfully aware that if I pulled away she would clamp down harder. In the midst of all of this, I could not help but notice Kip in the background trying to steal McKenzie's rabbit hurriedly dragging it across the wolf pen. This was a strange mix of pain and amusement. When the incident passed, it seemed more like a baby tantrum than a vicious act, yet I learned to respect Mckenzie's strength.

Home life has its problems. My neighbor complains about my animals and it becomes too stressful to stay. One of my friends offers me a cabin on her land. It is poor but will work. There is no insulation, no running water. It does have some electrical outlets. When I move I find out just how territorial wolves are. Mckenzie goes berserk. She tears around inside her new pen bouncing off the walls and soon jumps out over the eight-foot chain-link fence. This makes me extremely nervous. I have to keep McKenzie under control on the island. She is learning to hunt and she can't roam on her own looking for prey.

On top of the move, I am down with the flu. I am so sick that my community comes to help—people I love, people I like, people who do not like me . But we are community so they must come, as I have done for them, and as I will do again. Brenda brings food. Rayna brings a book. Ann brings talk. Several friends bury meshed wire in the ground and weave it together with the wire fence to secure the wolf pen. They also string the top with chicken wire so Mckenzie cannot jump out. Just before this occurs my friend Dan brings me some soup. Mckenzie leaps out of the pen and lands on the hood of Dan's truck. To see a wolf flying down from nowhere is spectacular. Dan is surprised. Mckenzie is afraid because I seldom have visitors, so she runs and hides.

Dan comes in for some of my bitter coffee. He pulls up an old battered chair and we talk. Dan and I often talk about being Indian because he is mixed-blood Chickasaw. He works with deer hide to make beautiful parfleches and shirts. His paintings are wonderful. He paints old-time scenes of his ancestors. Dan is proud of his blood. He wears his long blond hair down. His eyes are bright blue though his face and fea-

Photo: Beth Biggs

McKenzie and Teresa.

tures are Native. For some reason that disturbs some people as if Native people must all be generic stock, black-haired and dark-eyed, and copper-colored.

Dan calls me one day to go and collect a big doe that was hit by a car. He wants the hide for his parfleches but Mckenzie can have the meat. I am watching my neighbor's child, a little, sandy-haired boy, Baird. I take him with me. When we get to the doe, the boy tugs energetically at the carcass trying to help Dan put it in the Jeep. Dan is patient and shows the boy how to pull the hide off the legs with his hands, and the secret places where the skin is attached. Baird proudly helps Dan skin the

doe. We then drive back to Baird's house. Some of the neighbor children are there, two girls, Carey and Nari. They want to see the doe. One child says a beautiful thing, "T, do I look like that without my skin?" "Yes, Nari, you do."

There it is—the old dilemma. How do we make amends for the life that feeds us? Is it any wonder that many religions involved sacrifice? We feel guilty that we take life to live, but it is all around us in nature. But Nari touches the heart of the matter. It is all of us under the skin. I give the doe to McKenzie, noticing that milk still drips from the doe's teats. Somewhere a fawn is hungry and grieving.

Soon after, I call some Native Californians to ask more questions. I ask them about the old man I had seen on the mountain where I grew up. They tell me the mountain is considered sacred by some who live there. The old man had been traditional Native American and had gone up there to pray. He was not a cliché mystic. He was a kind old man who loved the mountain and the animals and plants there. That is mystical enough. I think that the most common things must be the most miraculous. He never said much to me, but I sensed that he was calm and happy. He belonged to that place and himself. He was rooted and comfortable. He was at peace with The Mystery. Because he was unafraid he did not claim to know it all or to control others. But what impressed me the most was that he *belonged* on that land.

Where do I belong? Not in Italy. My family has deserted that land. But that blood is close. The grounding in North America is the strongest for me. But I also notice Mckenzie is unconcerned about my ideas of blood and space. All she knows is that she feels comfortable living where she has been as a cub, as long as it doesn't change too much. And that she loves me.

I give my friend Penny my poems to type for my family. Later, she calls me. "Teresa, I think you should give these poems

to Rayna. She has a small press. I think she would like them." I tell her okay, but I don't really know what small presses are. In time, I will learn that they are the voice of the world. I write about Mckenzie in my poems.

On the mountain once while I rode The Corinthian, my gray gelding, a phrase fluttered into my head, *Learning from Eagle, Living with Coyote*. At that time, I had not written anything yet. It was years before I had moved to the island. But now I remember the phrase and realize it is the title for my book of poetry.

Rayna calls to tell me that she wants to make my poems into a book. She helps me with the editing of the handmade version of *Learning from Eagle*. She laughs kindly about my lack of knowledge about verb tenses. Then she says, "Teresa, you don't see time the way most people do." Later, I learned that not all editors think my sense of time is so endearing, only foolish. Their lives are so rapid they cannot see stories anymore. What is the most important—-the stories or the tenses? Or does it take more than one kind of person to make a book?

I admit I have trouble with time. I know in my heart that all times are one and time moves in a great circle. People are forcing themselves to live at a tremendous speed. What are they running from? If they go fast enough they still won't escape the dark. I love the slowest moments. The times when I ease into cool water on a hot day. When I wake with birds calling or wind blowing. When the snow falls at night and I look up and see the flakes dancing, spinning down like the milky way coming to live around me. No tenses or fences will keep me in.

So now I am becoming a storyteller, a writer.

Chapter Six

The Give-Away

The African lion from the rescue center was not the first predator who taught me about the give-away. When I was a child, about ten, walking in the twilight of the dusty summer country I met my first lion. I often crossed an old plank bridge whose creaky voice followed my footsteps. I would then climb the brown hillsides above the lake dotted with grand oak trees and scrawny scrub. One purple evening, the oaks standing silently in the cool, the peace was pierced by the scream of a mountain lion. It is a sound like the soul being torn from the body, designed to frighten listeners into a panic. A scream stimulates the start of a chase, or it is a call for the coming together to create new life.

I froze. But my heart like a deer's was already bounding away with the characteristic bounce that says, *I'm strong! Strong! STRONG! You'll never catch me.* The horses and deer taught it to me. Standing still, and slowly turning my head, I looked directly into Lion's piercing gaze. In that moment I felt the terror of impending death and the fascination of being so close to this beautiful big cat. Lion asked me something unspo-

ken. Her eyes and her posture asked me if I were ready to give-away. The moment was a great dark well with the light shining from far above. I spoke out loud to Lion with a child's pure courage: "I'm not ready to give you my life. You are hungry and it is a dry year, but I need my life. I want to live. My father had taught me to always talk to animals and let them know what is going on. I had to trust his wisdom in that moment.

Lion stood fifty feet from me, scarcely two jumps on broad swift paws. Lion's eyes were soft, almost like a priest or doctor with compassion for a dying patient. Lion stepped closer. The dusty yellow fur was touched with red: claws still sheathed. I could hear her soft slow panting breath.

I turned around and drew fragrant air deep into my lungs. I walked away. My feet moved as if I were wading through deep water, not knowing if Lion would release me. Lion's eyes were hot against my back. My blood pushed through my veins quickly and goose flesh covered my body. Ten strides. Twenty. I heard nothing. Not the soft running tread and then silence as a predator leaves the ground. No big claws caught my legs. No teeth bit the back of my head. I have seen deer carcasses with those fang marks.

Was Lion letting me go? Glancing back I saw that the tawny form had disappeared. Then my legs began to tremble, weakness hit me hard. Lion had let me live. Life is a great gift.

Lion taught me compassion because I was allowed to walk away. There are other powers in this world greater, stronger, faster than me. I am food to them. My body remembers this deep in my bones.

Mountain Lion showed me the asking and it is Lion's teaching that makes me

respect the deer's gift...the give-away. The question to be asked is: *Why is it that some must die to give others life?* The universe twinkles around us, swirling with the power that eats suns whole and drools out the gases that in turn become stars again. The world teaches us, but the truth is hard. If we fear to look we will never know. Coal was once forests. Diamonds were trees under pressure and heat, the volcano of Earth's heart. All life helps all life. Everyone sees the world as they are. If you see life as all things fighting then you will fight. If you see life as everything helping each other then that is how you will live.

The idea of the give-away is a comfort to me. To hunt is a sacred thing. You pray, you fast, you obey the rules. If you are a good person perhaps a deer or rabbit will hear you and give you their gift. Then you leave a gift for them after they're dead. You tell them why you need them and what you will do with them. It is very personal, respectful. You wish them a good journey and tell them that you, too, will lie cold and still on the ground one day and give yourself back to the Mother of us all. I don't know how I learned of the give-away. I must have heard it somewhere and it lodged in my soul.

As I sit in my cabin remembering Mountain Lion, I know Mckenzie must remember the hunt, the asking, and the give-away. I have to find living food for the young wolf. And eventually she must learn to kill a deer.

Beanie has already helped me by catching mice and rats for Mckenzie. She kills the rodent then drops it at Mckenzie's gray feet. I, too, begin to find and catch rabbits and other rodents for Mckenzie. The mice I catch I talk to. I tell them if they get out of the pen they are free. I ask for their forgiveness and explain our position. Poor mice. But I do see cleverness and wit under the most extreme odds. Once Mckenzie missed a mouse because the mouse kept so still. It then crept out of the wolf pen right behind the young wolf who sniffed and dug, but she never saw the smart rodent.

I am surprised to see that little animals fight back. In the woods beside the cabin, Mckenzie found a furious vole who bit her so hard on the lip that she dropped it. Beanie ran in to finish off the vole and then released its limp body. Mckenzie snapped it up. I wonder if the vole was valiant because it was not his time to give-away?

I tell people on the island I need meat to feed the wolves. My friend, Will, comes by one day. He is the director of the local arts center, a homegrown version of the opera, ballet, theater, art gallery, and art school. Will has a desert face with a hopeful attitude that water is close by. He has a healthy respect for the wolves ever since the day they insisted he climb out a window. Will was wolf sitting and had to climb up on a large trunk while the wolves suspiciously circled him. He finally crawled out a window. This time Will good naturedly finds himself chasing mice around a woodpile. He then releases them into the wolf pen for Mckenzie to catch herself.

Mckenzie studies the night shadows and chases the mice up the walls of my old cabin. She grows strong on our daily runs. She is also comfortable getting in and out of the Jeep. But the hunting is hard for her because she has only Peter, Beanie, and myself as pack mates.

One day I catch a rabbit and give it to her to kill. She grabs him quickly and in the right place at the waist to break his spine. But she takes too long and I fear the rabbit is suffering greatly. I run up to hit him between the ears. I see his face. He is not afraid. He is calm, peaceful even. In my own life, I have been seriously hurt and gone into shock. So I realize the greatness of the world that helps us to avoid pain and fear in the face of a terrifying death. But what was the rabbit trying to teach me? Was it that The Mystery has compassion for beings in trauma, and frees us from great suffering?

Mckenzie will not eat dog food, nor do I think she should. Getting a lot of meat all the time is difficult. My neighbor, Donna, calls one day and offers to give her old hens to Mckenzie, if I will help to butcher them. I walk over to Donna's hen house. "Let's take the hens into the woods so that the others don't have to see them die," says Donna. So, we carry the old hens gently in our arms, one by one, into the woods. I remember Granny's advice about butchering a chicken: *Look them in the eye*. I do, softly asking for forgiveness, then kill them with a hatchet while Donna holds them, her eyes bright. I kill for Mckenzie and bring her their bodies. They will be the only domestic meat she ever eats.

Mckenzie is strange about people. A person whom she had met as a pup she will show herself to, but they cannot touch her. They can only see her. A stranger might never know she lives in the pen. She has a den that she dug under a barberry bush. She also has a hiding place under my bed from where she can peer out at the world discreetly. The cabin is isolated and I discourage visitors. Wolves are naturally shy. And Mckenzie must retain her fear of people. In the wild if a wolf is sighted it is likely the wolf will be shot.

I still need to drive her around in the Jeep. It is the only way to get her into the mountains. So we work and live. Life feels vast and I am small. Am I doing the right thing by returning Mckenzie to her ancestors? I hear her howling. She hunts well in my mind's eye. I imagine her chasing the deer down the trail and turning her head to look smiling back at me.

At five months Mckenzie has terrible table manners. She gives clear meaning to the phrase, "Don't wolf your food." Watching her with a carcass even makes Peter come inside the cabin. There is a frenzy around food. Her face and ruff get bloody when she eats a deer carcass. She consumes everything, even cracking the bones to get at the marrow. But what I think is disgusting and what Mckenzie thinks is disgusting is quite different. Perhaps the grossest thing in the world for Mckenzie is to watch me eat bananas. She can't believe I'd put something like a banana in my mouth. Sometimes I tease her, putting a banana in front of her nose. She grimaces and pushes it away with her teeth.

The roadkill deer carcasses make for some interesting predicaments. One day Cherry started to sound sick going uphill, a combination of lack of power and an alarming choking sound. Whenever I have a little money saved, the car breaks down. I worry that the Jeep will collapse with Mckenzie in it. I don't know if Triple A will haul the wolves back to the cabin, and my prospects hitchhiking with wolves is dismal.

So my friend Will let me borrow his truck. He is proud of this truck and shows me all its features. I guess he considers it a very acceptable wolf vehicle. The truck has a camper shell. It is totally enclosed with room to spare. The wolves will drive in luxury in all that space. Within two days of borrowing the truck I drive down the road and there in the ditch under the salal is a

big fat doe, fresh roadkill. Taking roadkill deer is frowned upon by the law, but I pull over and leap out. I take a long cautious look first up and then down the road. Nobody in sight. Peter and Mckenzie smell the dead deer and begin to whine. I walk up to the doe and notice the little hooves and long, slender legs carved like madrona wood and now just as still. At least she had been killed outright, not condemned to a slow death. The doe will give-away.

Pulling on her front legs I slowly drag the doe closer to the truck and wonder how to get her into it. I look down the road again to see if anyone is coming. There is. A serious bicyclist. With his cone-shaped helmet and bright-red bike pants, he looks like he has fallen from outer space. Perhaps this man will help. Without help I will never get her into the truck by myself. But what if this guy does not understand? Here he comes, whipping up the road like the wind. He pulls over, and grandly gets off his bike.

"Well, we're too late," he says. I stare at him, curiously. "Too late for what?" "She's dead," he replies. I look more closely at him, and then at the lifeless, stiffening doe. The wolves are strangely silent. "Oh, she's dead all right," I say, "but…uh… I'd kinda like to put her into this truck." The man is clearly mystified. He removes his helmet. "You want to bury her?" I look him in the eye. "You from off island?" "Yeah." *Great!* I think. *If he tells anyone they'll think he is nuts.*

"Well," I say, "I need your help. I want to take this deer home and skin her." The man nods. "You make rugs or something?" "Not exactly. Could you help me pull her up and into the truck?" I smile. The man props up his bicycle and grabs a hoof. Together we pull the deer easily, but as we get closer the vehicle begins to rock violently. Whining and snarling echoes from the interior. The man stops, alarmed. "Lady, you got some big dogs?" He looks at me hopefully. The snarling gets louder.

Most people would know by the sounds that whatever is in that truck is big, feral, and hungry. Mckenzie is spooking inside the canopy because of the nearness of the stranger.

"Well, they're not really dogs." The man grows still. "What are they?" "Actually, they're wolves." "Wolves?" the man says with a mock bravado. "You have wolves in that truck and we're going to put this deer in there?" "Well, put is the wrong word," I tell him. "We'll have to throw her in very quickly." "Oh?" says the man, his eyebrows arching. "I can't have them leaping out and eating it here! I'd never get them back in the truck till they were done. That would be bad." "Oh," repeats the man. In both our minds is the picture of wolves having a picnic spread out on the road.

"But won't your truck be a mess when you get home?" he offers. "Ah, no! I'll drive real fast so they'll be skittering around back there. They won't be able to get hold of her, and I can always hose out the truck." The man takes a deep breath and steps up to the deer. Grasping the front hooves and gesturing for him to do the same with the back, we pull the doe up close to the truck.

"I'll count 'one, two, three,' then we'll heave her in." The man nods, his hands move skittishly on the cold stiff legs. "Don't stick your hands too far in," I warn. I don't want him to scare Mckenzie, but the bicyclist must wonder for the safety of his limbs. Throwing open the back of the truck, we heave in unison and it is done. The wolves, frantic for their carcass, grab it, and pull it quickly inside. The bicyclist glimpses lolling tongues and large fangs fastening on the dead doe. The scene resembles a horror movie.

I slam the back of the truck closed and run for the cab. A furious snarling arises from the back, deepened by the canopy.

The man cocks his head, "No one is going to believe this." As I speed away, I yell out the window, "I know!"

Inside the truck the wolves claw, scrambling for a foothold. Behind me the bicyclist stands with hands raised to the sky, shaking his head. An enigma. All of us provide a window to The Mystery. That's all right, friend on the bicycle, someone did the same to me. In a little drugstore in Half Moon Bay, a wild person with long, swinging black hair walking backwards, stared with a half grin. He was Native and he stared at me a long time smiling. When I looked at his bright face something in me woke like the slap of rain on an uneasy sleeper. I've been waking up ever since. I think this person was Coyote.

When we get home I have a hard time getting the carcass out of the truck. The wolves pull one way and I another. Once I get the deer out of the truck, I open the belly with my skinning knife for Mckenzie. She eats all of the insides first, then she starts on the meat. She even eats the head. Mckenzie eats like she has never been fed. She eats until her stomach swells like the full moon. Then she lies by the dead deer or flops around it, drunk from eating so much. Later she makes a scrape in the wolf pen and partially buries her food. Then bit by bit it disappears.

Kip loves this turn of events. I have quit trying to keep him inside the wolf pen. He climbs out each evening and hunts small rodents, insects, and slugs. This all comes to him quite naturally. But the sight of his little body earnestly trying to carry a deer leg that Mckenzie has dropped is amusing. If Kip has his way, he pees on all the food so the others won't eat it. In the early days, Kip peed on all the dog dishes, so I had to separate him from the others at mealtime.

Kip eats everything: grapes, sunflower seeds, deer hooves, Beanie's collar. He is not very particular. One day Kip swallowed an enormous yellow slug. He gagged a couple of times and passed out. The slug was stuck in his throat and he couldn't breathe. Frantically I tried to pull the slug from his throat but my fingers couldn't get a grip. If he didn't breathe soon he'd die. An inspiration came to me. With my finger I pushed the slug gently down his throat. I hoped it would move down his esophagus and not down his trachea. I hoped that the pressure would not rupture anything that would cause Kip harm. The slug moved down as far as my finger could reach. Kip was very still, not breathing. Mckenzie crept up and whined. I massaged him in my hands and every now and then blew air down his nose. The

little black body lay limp and unresponsive. I stopped, thinking that he was dead, he was so still in my hands. My tears slid down and splashed on his fur. Kip, the little comic, how could he be gone? Did he give-away?

Beanie barked, and Kip suddenly stirred, coughed, and stood up. He looked me in the eye, shook himself, leapt down, and trotted away as though nothing had happened. I never saw him eat a yellow slug again.

If I try to put Kip in his box at night he cries. The thin tearing sound is plaintive and soulful. He is a good hunter. One morning I wake up and Kip is staring at me. His bright beady eyes are expressive, but this look I cannot fathom. He makes me

feel lonely. There are no foxes on the island so Kip will have no mate here. He will never know the joy of having a good partner and do the wild joyous runs that foxes do when they court. Kip cannot stay on the island.

While watching him in the dusty morning sunlight it strikes me that it is now time for Kip to go. As he grew, he became shyer and I did not think he would come up to anyone but me. His shyness would give him a better chance in the wild. And he hunted with ease. Studying my map I decide to take him to a national park where there are other foxes and plenty of food.

Before the morning ends, we are ready for the journey. I put Kip in his box, get in my car, and head for the park. The forest there is deep and dark. There is a lake and it beckons us through the trees as we hike up trails. The wolves follow me merrily as I carry Kip's box, looking for the best spot to release him. I want to get him far enough into the wilderness before opening his box. Because Kip is a loner, it could be difficult to catch him once he was out.

Deep into the forest, I reach a spot that feels right. It is near a familiar lake and I know from previous hikes in this area that there are many foxes. I sit down to eat my lunch and I open Kip's box. The wolves press up close to steal food. But the little fox surprises me. I thought he would stay awhile and visit, maybe beg for grapes, which are his favorite. But Kip gives me one sympathetic look and with a rational flick of his white-tipped tail scurries out of sight. He must have known.

The wolves and I sit there in the silence. Holding back tears, I try to eat. The wolves manage to make off with a banana that they don't eat; and a peanut butter bread crust, which Peter eats and Mckenzie grimaces at. Kip does not return. At sunset we drive back to the island to be lonely for a while. In my memory I hold the picture of Kip and his little black eyes dancing with sympathy. I must not be sad, Kip has chosen life. But his soft release makes me think of Mckenzie's impending release, but her risk will be the greater.

Kip's freedom reminds me that we must find our way back to the center of the world to stand on the peak, arms raised, palms open, and cry into the circling wind. We want our spirits back. They were stolen and here we are, naked empty orphans. We must be able to dance at full moon and sing together songs that we've made. We must learn from the wolves who do not care if you are tundra or timber or what color your pelt. I must read the riddle of sympathy in a fox's eyes.

There is a scarlet wasp that lives in between my curtain and the wolf-smudged window. There is also a dusky brown spider that stalks my walls. I watch them hunt, as skillful as a puma, as swift as the little falcon. They are small wildernesses that comfort the tameness of my walls. I risk their sting and bite. But I trust that they know where they are and where I sleep, below their little jungles.

Do I go live in the wilderness or do I create community wildness and form my own pack? Are we any different in emotion and thought from the people who lived before us? Have we just traded dreams?

Kip was sympathetic because my choice is hard.

Chapter Seven

She Calls My Secret Name

The old man whom I had met on the mountain many years ago had called me "tsimmu." I have since found a book about Native Americans indigenous to California that included what I thought was this word. It is part of a longer name that means, "dreams of a wolf." Tsimmu became my second name. In time I learned that most Native tribes have naming ceremonies. It is not unusual for a person to have four names: a childhood name, a name given by yourself or by an elder, a secret name, and a name as an elder. There is something very powerful in a name—-with a name you can capture something or you can release it.

I dreamed of a wolf
my name
my name.
I dreamed of a wolf.
Grandfather leans over,
he whispers,
"When the wolves sleep,
they dream of tsimmu."

When we hunt I think of myself as tsimmu. In the wild Mckenzie is giving up the name I gave her. It seems the wild animals need no names. They recognize each other in a silence that is more profound than speech. Mckenzie can rivet me with her piercing intelligent gaze. In the wild Mckenzie becomes my guide through the thick woods. She is my teacher now as she shows me the world. She becomes a meditation as she stalks after a mouse or a rabbit. I watch for her black-tipped tail moving in front of me. When I howl she comes. But when it is time to return home to the island, she is reluctant to get into the Jeep. I dare not think too far ahead. Mckenzie and I will be parted. And if Mckenzie refuses to come back with me, and I leave her too early she will starve. If she really does not want to get into the Jeep, I cannot force her.

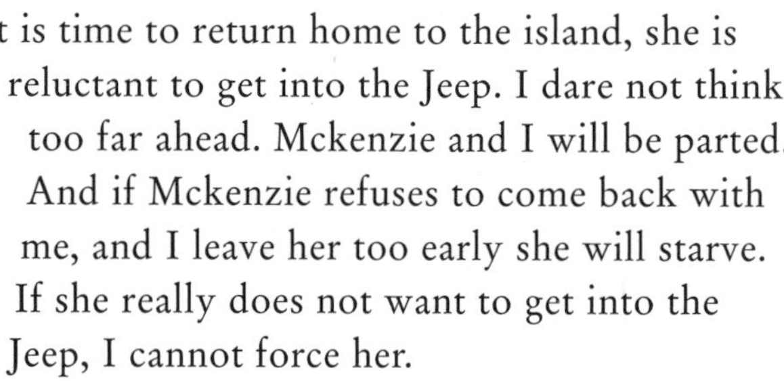

I must decide where Mckenzie should be released. Too far north and the wolves are even more persecuted and the weather is much harsher. In a popular national park, if Mckenzie is sighted the park authorities will create too much of a stir. In wilderness areas there will be hunters. I fear the shoot-and shovel-theory practiced by people who kill predators and hide the evidence. There are those who do not look at predators as teachers but as competitors. There should be an adequate population of wolves in Mckenzie's new home. Too many wolves means fighting and not enough game. If there are too few wolves Mckenzie will have no pack. Wolf packs can vary from four to ten animals usually, and even as many as thirty. But in the lower forty-eight states the wolf is so persecuted that a small pack is most likely what will be available.

Since Mckenzie is learning to hunt in the wild while on the island I have to watch her closely so she will not hunt livestock.

I am careful not to let her eat tame food. I definitely do not want her to get a taste now. Mckenzie needs to know that the real world for her is the place that is called "wilderness." I wonder often about the word and what it means. The meanings in my thesaurus and dictionary are not very good. Wilderness has many bad connotations. Wilderness equals dangerous and unpredictable in a world suffocated by illusions of safety. There is risk, there is death.

We need more good words. The one good word derived from wilderness is "free." On a long rope or in a pen Mckenzie is the opposite of free. But what is freedom? Freedom in a wolf pack means there are rules to be followed for the good of the pack. Wolves must think of one another in the wild.

There is a paradox in this mystery, the bittersweet call that draws you close to the cliff. Looking down you could be swept away in a heartbeat by the sight of all that space. Then be dead to this life. I once told my Mother that if I had to live any other way, other than the free life I have now, I would lay my life down. My mother brokenly said, "That is hard for a mother to understand—-you walk to music I cannot hear." And Mother! I cannot explain it!

Is it the fear of death, of cold, of loneliness, and of hunger that keeps people from living? The fear made of *What if.... What if I die?* You will. So live. I have called Death and when Death came it helped me shoulder my life joyfully. When I am close to the dark I look again into the eyes of Lion and find solace. I have felt the shock that saves the body from pain when injured. I trust that The Mystery gave us this gift out of compassion. This gives me hope that The Mystery is beneficent, and the plan, whatever it may be, is going as it should.

I have seen the deer fawn die gently of surprised soft shock in the jaws of a wolf. I see the grass come back every spring and the sun warm the land in summer. Here is the great circle written out before us. There is dust and dust. The dust of stars that makes up our bodies and the land. The dust of a myriad of little dead things: insects, plants, old fallen trees, and tiny chips of bone. My horses roll in this powder of mortality and stars. And I curry it up from their backs, and deeply breathe it in.

How wonderful this dance we live! We shall never be bored with all this changing! I make my life up out of talk and bread, and laugh at it. It is all right to die. Look around. See? The world shows me how. Here is the circle. Now live. The world tells me

"Take your food with compassion
and it will give itself to you gently.
Look at the plants and animals and people
and not only feel their pain, joy, fear and healing
but become them. Really, you already are
the geese traveling north to tundra,
the soft secret slug under the fern,
the red calf in the pen,
the little stallion, pawing impatiently, waiting to be put to death
because he's lame. Be happy he is not lame in the heart.
The new flowers and ancient trees in the Hoh,
Yellow corn growing in the garden,
A woman writing wild.
You are all of these."

To be safe, parents tell their children, *Go this way or that.* They must. We will always deny risk and the dark that surrounds those we love. We preserve life in salt and sugar and maybe life should go to ground, like Kip, to raise a family. Death is only the dark creating place of the womb. All roads lead deep into Earth and The Mystery hides behind leaf mulch and maggots. Nature is incredibly designed for balance. If you see the tension between Life and Death not as a battle but as a balance, then it is softer, gentler. Nature shows us that things come back, and sometimes

gives back with great compassion. Turn around, part the brush. Sometimes the elk calf hides safely in silence and even Lion Woman cannot find her. Fox cubs play in dusty sunlight and Golden Eagle screams before she swoops, giving them a chance to learn, to live.

My horses allow me to ride, to be four-legged again. The wolves bring me mice and deer legs, leaving them sweetly at my door then backing up to watch with compassionate yellow eyes. Empathy opens the twisted gate. The Mystery is all of us and we are learning. One day we will understand. The night reaches out to embrace me and the stars lie on my skin like the hottest coals. I am alive. I have stories to tell. I am so lucky.

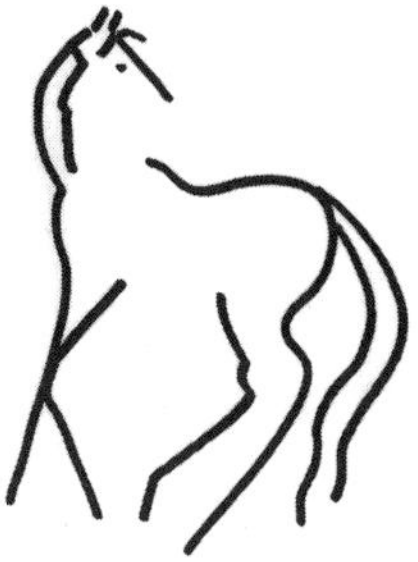

Stories belong to tribes. Friends from the Blackfeet reservation told me this story freely and I pass it on, (but not the whole story). I write it with the understanding that it really should be told orally and by the right person at the right time. Here is the story:

A woman was captured on a raid by a neighboring tribe. Perhaps she was out looking for herbs. I like to think she was caught because she was the type of person who wants to stand in a high place and look out over the vast golden vistas of the grassland.

But she was captured and brought back along the trail towards a strange village. Somehow along the way she managed to escape. I imagine her running, her long braid swinging and sharp ears listening for pursuit. Perhaps it was by some bluff or tree line that she saw the dark hole that led deep underground. She threw herself onto her hands and knees and then on her belly pulled herself in.

It was probably May, the month when most wolves have their cubs. And in the deep den there flashed golden eyes of what the white cattlemen call the loafer wolf—-the pale hunter of buffalo. The Plains wolf. The woman was frightened of her pursuers and so talked to the wolf mother and perhaps wolf father of her need. Silently they watched her, already knowing her intent by feel and smell. The wolves allowed her to stay, the story goes, and they brought her meat as they would their own kind.

I wasn't told how long the woman stayed with the wolves but at some point a band of her own people found her and took her back to their camp. She told the amazing story to her tribe. There was disbelief at her tale. So she took her people to the wolf den, but not so close that her wolf benefactors would be afraid. She called her wolf companions up close and decorated them with red paint and eagle feathers, which she tied in their thick fur. Then, when her people saw this they believed her and honored the wolves.

I was not told if the woman went back to the camp or lived out her life with the wolf pack. There are many Native people with wolf in their name. Wolf Child is one I am fond of.

In between road trips I must regularly exercise the wolves. I have had to figure out ways to run with them and to stay clear of civilization. To run on the island with the wolves is not relaxing. These are not casual outings to listen to the chuckling of birds or to watch black noses at the ground and outstretched bushy tails scamper through the summer pines. Instead, I am always watching for their safety as well as mine. Oftentimes, we run at night to avoid people.

Mckenzie only ran loose when she was a pup. One time when she was a four-month old pup she got out of her pen. I knew she had gotten away because a neighbor ran by with her child under her arm shouting, "The wolf is loose, the wolf is loose." It sounded like the Apocalypse. Running with Mckenzie and Peter grows more difficult because the island is shrinking. Sadly, the island is quickly developing a larger population so I

cannot let the wolves roam. And there seems to be no changing what is happening. The land is disappearing.

I used to tie Mckenzie to Peter and they ran together as a team. I had to make a couple of tackles when she got away from Peter. Mckenzie would run towards me, tongue lolling, all ready to dodge. Crouching, I knew that if I missed, there would be no second chance. Then, swoosh! I'd fly down on top of Mckenzie and we would roll together in the grass as she good naturedly gnawed my hands. Then, one day Mckenzie became stronger than Peter and while running, flipped poor Peter on his back and dragged him a few yards. After that I could not tie them together since Peter made it clear he did not like it.

Peter comes when called so he is allowed to run loose. But I had to start running Mckenzie on a separate long rope. She can run far faster than me. If I have her on the long line we resemble a chariot race. Once I was dragged out into the pond and got tangled under a tree so that I almost drowned. I came up with muddy hair and handfuls of reeds. I sputtered so loudly that Mckenzie spooked and off we went again.

In winter, I go out on the ice with the wolves. Their bright happiness and splayed-out toes and legs are comedic. Then quicker than I think possible, they manage to tear off along the ice, their legs working like pistons. With a look of alarm I run as fast as I can, holding onto the rope, and fearful of the moment

Peter (left) and Mckenzie at the cabin.

when the rope pulls taut and the hundred-pound wolf keeps running at twenty-five-miles per hour. I hit the ice, belly down, but I dare not let go of the rope.

Wolves need to howl as much as humans need to talk and sing. They howl for a variety of reasons: If they want to draw the pack together or if they want to communicate from one pack to another. When they howl in the wild perhaps they are discussing where the game is, or what is happening on the land. When Mckenzie howls to me in the wilderness it has a plaintive sound, almost as if she's asking, *Where are you?* On the island, Mckenzie and Peter often will howl as a means to get me up in the morning. Sometimes they will go into their crawl space under the cabin, directly under my bed, and howl. Their howling is deafening at close range, so they get me moving with no difficulty at all. They also howl for territorial reasons and just for the pure joy of singing. Mckenzie's high-pitched pup howl has matured into a melodic mezzo-soprano with a dark medium quality. When Peter, Mckenzie, and I howl together, our voices harmonize.

No one can see inside my Jeep because it has tinted windows. But when the wolves howl, it draws a crowd. Even one howling wolf can create a crowd. In the beginning, it was funny to watch people look around the small grocery parking lot for the source of the howls, bewildered when all they saw was my Jeep.

Driving and howling now seem natural. However, when my mom comes to visit she often asks, "Why do people stare at your car?" Mom is funny. Perhaps the way we grew up makes it normal for her daughter to have wolves in the car. She tries not to notice them. The wolves love Mom, like cats who go near those people who are not particularly attracted to them. Once at my

sister-in-law's baby shower, mom called them her "grand wolves." Then she told the guests about how the wolves had brought a road-killed porcupine into the house, and how, unfortunately, I sat on it in the dark. (The wolves had lovingly put it on my chair). My sister-in-law's family never asked me to baby sit after that.

On our wilderness weekend jaunts the wolves and I are free, far from the worries of life on the island. Perhaps this is what it must have been like for the ancestors when they roamed among the wild animals. The wolves are often out of my sight and sound when we hike, but they always come back to check on my whereabouts. Perhaps they wonder at the slowness of their comrade on two legs. I am in awe of their acute senses. They read the trail with their noses and can feel the emotions of these scents.

On the paths through the woods, hunting with the wolves, another me walks. My hair grows longer and I do not tie it up. I imagine my eyes can see in the dark like an owl's. And silence squeezes from my pores like water weeping from stone. The blackberry bushes take hairs from me that I suppose the birds will use later. Walking slowly and watching carefully, I think of the deer and their narrow slotted hooves. Step...pause...step...breathe. Look! Don't slap at the twigs that grab and poke, stroke them aside and soon they dance with my movements and gracefully let me pass. Mckenzie does these things naturally. Peter and Mckenzie jog together on their path, shoulders touching, nosing the wind. My thoughts chase each other as we roam the paths through wilderness.

While walking to a lake I see a big mule deer outlined in the silver moonlight. The deer's jaws glide back and forth as he chews. Then he stops as though thinking, and watches, softly swinging his great ears forward. Looking down at Mckenzie I see that she is crouched, intently struggling with some inner conflict. She looks questioningly up at me, as if asking, *That's what we've been eating?* The buck carries a massive rack. It is important that Mckenzie is not afraid, but the buck could kill her. I stalk a couple of steps and the buck freezes. He must be thinking, *Hmm, are they serious?* Peter follows me. There is no other sound but the night wind that circles around us, mixing the smell of green leaves and earth and water. Mckenzie needs to chase the buck, I need to initiate a pursuit.

Dashing at the buck who glares, surprised at my charge, the deer then whirls and runs through the bush. Peter gallops after him. I wave at Mckenzie who follows after Peter but then turns and looks at me strangely. I whisper at her, my childhood brush voice born again in that moment, "Go on, go on." Mckenzie turns and runs between the dark shapes of the trees, following Peter into the night. She understands the chase.

And I stand there alone. The breeze comes up and lifts my hair, tossing it wildly. In the distance, I hear the retreating gallop of the deer and the brush rustling against my wolves. A part of me runs with her and I hear the old man of my childhood say, "All of us have a secret name...that is what the world calls us." I hear my name.

The Gray One and I are going back.

Chapter Eight

Hungry Water

Mckenzie paces by the fence. A slim gray shadow on big soft paws that are now as large as my hand. She whistles faintly, a high-pitched whimper, telling me she wants to go outside. The sound pulls gently on my heart. The island is my home but my prison as well. Mckenzie longs for our secret days spent in the mountains hunting, our real life. At home in the cabin we sit dreaming of reality. But I must work the horses to buy food, earn money to put gas in Cherry so we can drive to the real world, the wilderness. I cannot be gone longer than a couple of days at a time.

Loneliness seeps in. I hold back from telling anyone about life with the wolf in the mountains. The distance this puts between me and other people begins to shine out of my eyes. When I look at my reflection in the cracked windowpane of my cabin, I see the loneliness standing silent with the fir trees beyond. It is the look that the Gray One wears when she lifts her nose into the wind to read the breeze. Perhaps it is better not to talk about it. I am not sure it would be understood. Sometimes when I sit in the cabin it seems like I am dreaming this, but my body remembers those moments in the hills at the base of snow-covered peaks. I cherish my life.

Mckenzie is growing tall and getting whiter. Her coat has the long top fringe of an older wolf, her long mane hairs extend around her neck and down her back. Her black-saddle mark is striking against the white. When she is excited or angry all the hairs on her mane stand up, making her look even bigger. Long fangs show beneath her lips even when her mouth is closed. Mckenzie's emotional ability has grown with her size. When she is angry her eyes blaze with intensity, her lips wrinkle up baring fierce teeth, and her powerful growl commands respect.

Mckenzie still sleeps on the bed with me. Oftentimes she takes my hand or foot in her mouth and softly, gently, chews and nibbles—her gesture of affection. Too often she generously leaves little presents in my bed. One morning I rolled over, still drowsy, and touched what felt like maple leaves. A few minutes later I was awake and turned on my flashlight. Under my cheek like a love note was the clammy ear of a deer.

In the wild, Mckenzie has hunted and killed and there is no way of undoing her knowledge of that mystery. It makes it impossible for her to stay with me in the domestic setting of the island. She has now tasted warm life and hungers for it. And the wind in her heart is blowing stronger with every trip we make. It blows into me as well. Peter no longer goes with us. I am afraid Peter will start to hunt along with Mckenzie. And if the two wolves went off together and did not return, I may have no way of retrieving Peter. He is only half wolf, eight years old, and I am not sure he could survive in the wild. So, Peter and Beanie mourn at the cabin while Mckenzie and I are away.

The key to Mckenzie's return to the wild is to find the deer and elk and other wolves. Up till now, she has only caught rabbits and many small rodents. Her hunting improves. Now, when she chases some small quick rodent the twisting and dodging of

the little creature does not fool her a bit, and she anticipates the turns and ends up with a meal. She looks for food on her own and follows gullies and water with a rational stare. Her laughing mouth panting, she looks back at me with bright and merry golden eyes that say, *Keep up, will you!*

When I was ten I read *Born Free* by Joy Adamson. I read that book so many times that I finally took it to my mother and father one morning and said sadly, "What will I do if I wear the book out?" Pop looked up from his breakfast of fresh shad roe

McKenzie (front) and Peter at the cabin.

that he had caught and cooked, and said, "Why, it won't wear out because you'll memorize that book and take good care of it." Years later this book often returns to my thoughts, especially when I am roaming the mountains with Mckenzie. There are many parallels between the lioness and the young wolf.

Fall approaches and the weather slows down to breathe before changing. The colors in the maple leaves become warm with yellow and rusty red. The green leaks into the earth to wait for the circle to come round again. An idea comes to me and picks like a hen outside the edges of my brain. Mckenzie is nearly seven months old now. She needs to go out and stay for a few days by herself so she can get used to being alone. Perhaps she will call to one of the few wolves who hunts in that territory. This will be a weaning process for both of us. My mother said, "A parent's job is to teach the child to live without them. You are a successful parent when the child no longer needs you"

So on one of our weekend trips I decide the time is right to leave Mckenzie on her first extended education in the northern mountains. While she is off exploring for the day, I hike swiftly down the mountain drawing breath deep into my lungs. This feels necessary yet I feel so sad because she trusts me and I am betraying her trust. As I drive home, I clutch at a piece of her shedded fur. I want to hold on to that last moment of being with her. Anything could happen now. This could be the final release. Emotion swirls thick in my heart and I wonder if I am leaving her to die.

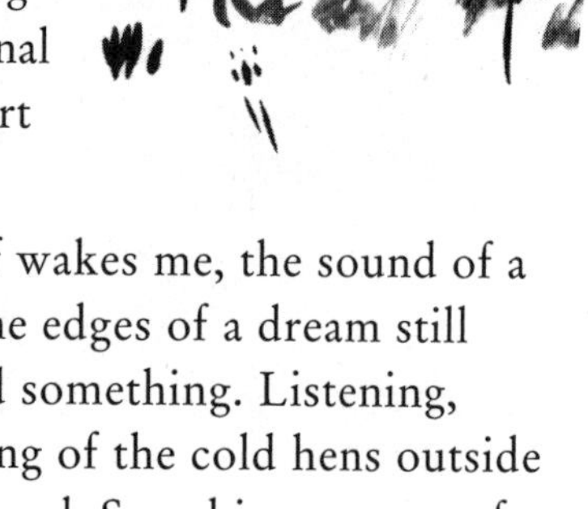

Rain on the cabin's aluminum roof wakes me, the sound of a continuous ocean wave. I lie in bed, the edges of a dream still tickling my consciousness. I had heard something. Listening, there is only the clucking and scratching of the cold hens outside the cabin's door. But that is not the sound. Searching memory for the mournful cry that hangs in my mind between waking and sleeping, I realize it is Mckenzie howling. But it couldn't be!

The rain fills my mind with drumming. Peter whines softly as I pat him. "It'll be fine, Pete." Slowly getting up, I turn on the light to reassure myself. Walking over to the big wood stove, I open it, and prod the fire. Peter follows me. The wood smells musty in the cold damp cabin. The chill taps my joints. The fall is turning into winter. It is the time of looking within, of wisdom. I look at the half wolf. "She has to spend time out there by herself, Pete. How else will she get acquainted with the land and the

other wolves?" Peter wags his tail slowly and he whines again.

Rain falls fiercely. The lights dim then go out. I stand in the dark like a carving, peering through the cracked window smeared by the rain and Mckenzie's nose. Wind moves out over the fir trees and turns the corner outside my door. Cold. It is six in the morning. A dull nervousness creeps like damp moss, spreading a wet chill. A cold kiss of warning. The wind picks up, tugging harder at the dark firs.

Beanie lies quietly watching me. Peter whines again, standing by the cabin door. Something is wrong. My bones feel uneasy. The weather grows worse. I begin to let myself think of Mckenzie in the mountains, living through her first storm alone. Is that it? Is that why the center of my chest has curled up into a tight fist? No, it isn't that. Mckenzie and I had been through bad weather before. We got caught earlier this fall up the side of a mountain with the rain falling, thinking about becoming snow. The wind was piercing on that trip, but Mckenzie was fine with her thick insulation of wool. The human body knows the seasons, accepting the weather, living with the time of rain and snow and wind. Seasons echo the earth, climb through legs and arms, turn hair white and trace rivers through faces. There is no fear of Grandmother, but something is wrong.

Is the young wolf going hungry? I test that thought, roll it around in my mind, then toss it out. No. Mckenzie has been hunting for several months, successfully. And always, when we hiked, I cached dog food for her. I knew there were no guarantees that McKenzie would get back in the Jeep to return to the island after one of our trips to the mountains. She knew where these supplies were, but she would only eat them if she was very, very hungry. Again, Peter whistles his sad whine, and slowly wags his brush of a tail as he catches my glance.

Granny comes into my mind. My mother's mother from the Ozarks. She had once told me that she knew before if anything

was going to happen to family. I was seven years old, sitting in her kitchen, the warm sweet smell of blackberry jam curled around us. Grandpa was outside in the garden fiddling with the onions. Granny was pouring boiling water over the jars. Paraffin melted in a pan mixed the smell of crayons with the blackberries.

"What would happen, Granny?" I asked. Granny turned, put the kettle on the stove, and wiped her hands on her apron; bristling red hair and smooth gnarled skin. "Life things, Teresa Ann." "But, how would you know?" I persisted. "I'd know," she said, looking out the window at Grandpa, her apron stained by the red blood of the blackberries. That was the feeling I had, the one that Granny had spoken of. Mckenzie, somehow, teeters on the thin path of life and her fear blows into my dreams. This is what I feel is wrong.

Outside the storm grows with rain and great winds. Rain has fallen for four days. I am not sure if the ferries are running, let alone the condition of the roads to the northern mountains. It will take two or three days to get back to Mckenzie.

Peter looks at me, then faces the door. Quickly, I fill my backpack with food, extra clothes, water, matches, and fire starter, all wrapped tightly in plastic. I put on my rain gear and boots. My actions tell Peter and Beanie what I have decided. We open the creaking cabin door and rush to the Jeep. Rain comes down so hard it distorts my hearing and blinds me. Yet, I also feel the rain's gentleness wrapped around this ferocity and power. Wind whips down and blows back the tops of the

trees, bending them until they groan. The horses in the pasture stand in the open, necks down, waiting for the weather to turn.

I load my gear into the Jeep. Peter and Beanie jump in the back. One last glance at my cabin. A lazy tendril of smoke creeps out of the pipe chimney. A sudden gust grabs it and the smoke vanishes in the fierce wind. Inside my chest a wolf howls to pack mates.

The island roads are strewn with branches and the odd bit of paper or cardboard. The wind increases. At the ferry dock I am amazed by the size of the waves. The crests break, rear, then fly off as spray in the wind like white-mane horses running across a dark-wet prairie. The boats buck at the dock.

We get on the ferry by timing the swells. The boat moves heavily. The ferryman waves and I rev the Jeep and race on to the deck. The big ferry starts the journey, rocking the way a green horse gallops. We cross the Sound to another island and wait near her shore for some change in wind or sea that I, not a boat person, could only guess at. Peter and Beanie sleep through it all. They are with me, and that is all that matters. We wait.

Because I ride horses Cross Country, jumping over solid obstacles at high speed, I had to learn to be instinctive. The horse and I run by feel; a trust in thick sinew and hooves like stone. It can be a wild, impersonal gaiety that comes in the galloping if you accept your own death. Now, my instincts say, *Get to the mountains. Concentrate on that.* The ferry crawls across the Sound ducking back and forth. On the mainland dock, we again time our movement and follow the other cars to the freeway going north.

My windshield wipers flap furiously at the rain. But the water is coming so fast the wipers do little good. I feel like racing, but I cannot. I remind myself that I am the only one who can go to Mckenzie. On the highway we make better speed, but the wind and rain make it impossible to drive over forty. The

radio plays '60s rock 'n' roll about sunshine and slow rivers of muddy water.

The river of my childhood was on the little ranch we owned before Pop got sick. We had built a house and a barn the first summer, and that winter we almost lost both. There was an incredible rainfall. One morning I awoke to a roaring outside my bedroom window. Jumping out of bed, my bare feet cold against the wooden floor, I pushed back the blue-flowered curtains my mother had made and peered through the window. The river was out of its bed, scarcely twenty feet away.

I padded to the kitchen where Pop stood staring. "Pop?" He turned to face me, steam wafting up from his coffee cup. "Yes, I know. I didn't want to wake you. It'll be all right." How did Pop know that? As a child, I marveled at the mystery of adulthood. We stood before disaster, and Father waited, watching, amber eyes calm. His russet hand held the cup lightly as he sipped the hot sweet coffee. I rested under his stillness like the elk calf in deep cover. There was safety in the silence of the brush, even as we watched whole trees float by on the flood. We saw a piece of what looked like a barn. *The water is hungry*, I thought. All that day we watched until evening when the river finally subsided.

We had luck. The house did not wash away from its place by the line of old oaks. I walked in the new riverbed, water recently drained, sand swept clean like rolled-out pie dough. There were new dead snags to explore, and tracks of animals stood out clearly. Caught on the snags were carcasses of the unfortunate, drowned in the flood. Bones soon to be picked clean by coyotes and buzzards. I respected the river after that. She is strong.

Thoughts of McKenzie bring me back to the present. Driving along the highway, I feel as if the world rolls along, while I in the red Jeep hang motionless. The dogwood, alder, and maple have shreds of color still clinging to them in the gray morning light—pale yellow and tired orange, red like dried blood. The wind will soon tear away the last leaves of autumn from the branches of the sleeping trees.

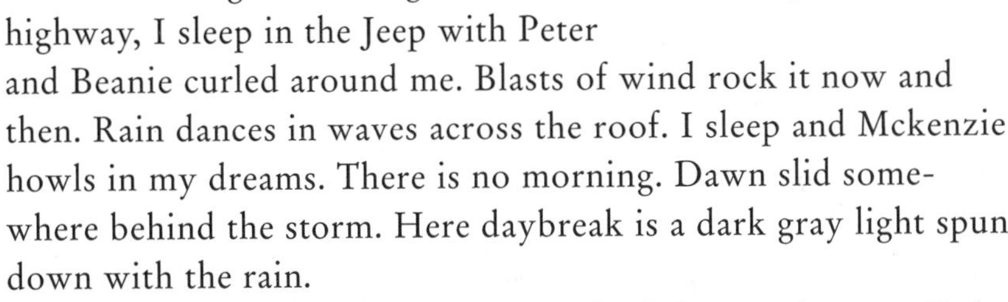

The day drove into night. I needed rest. Parking at a truck stop where a little restaurant clings to the edge of the highway, I sleep in the Jeep with Peter and Beanie curled around me. Blasts of wind rock it now and then. Rain dances in waves across the roof. I sleep and Mckenzie howls in my dreams. There is no morning. Dawn slid somewhere behind the storm. Here daybreak is a dark gray light spun down with the rain.

Peter and Beanie get out to pee. I feed them and pour a little water from my thermos into a small bowl for them. Back in the Jeep we drive on, and my companions settle to the rhythm of traveling. I buy more coffee with cream and sugar at the truck stop, sweet like Pop's as he watched the hungry water. Thoughts of the past and the cup warm my fingers and soul as I drive. Coffee reminds me of jumping horses cross country in competition. On those early mornings when you face a tough course, the simple pleasure of sweet coffee or tea is comforting. It also reminds me of Pop. Now I face the river, alone. But that is the job of parenthood, to teach you to stand by yourself.

Finally, the six-lane highway becomes a two-lane road. The rain continues to fall hard in big drops. The mountain's heart blood is next to us, and the flooding river of my memory still flows loud and dangerous. The racing river is the color of light chocolate now and the roar of its torrent drowns out the prickly drumming sound of the rain. Turning off the little two-lane highway, the road becomes a country lane winding around the base of the mountains. Intermittent yellow and black signs appear, warning, "Road Closed Ahead." The road keeps shifting, going one way then another as the mountains direct its course. I am forced to drive slower.

A thought rises like a fish. *If you're stopped what will you say?* This thought swims free for a moment, and then an answer rises alongside it. *I'm looking for my dog. My Alaskan tundra dog I lost while hiking.* Then a picture drifts into my mind, smooth against the bumpy road. I see myself walking with Mckenzie frisking beside me. A man in green appears suddenly, and says, "Jeeesus, lady! That's a wolf !" The man's face looks angry.

I think of the old man. Although I have talked to as many Native people as I could to learn more about my background, this Native man from my childhood continues to speak to me. Again, my feet stand on the red earth of the summer country with the old oaks and manzanita, the toyon berries and circling red-tailed hawks. Somehow an older me is driving in the rain, looking for something. But at the same time, I am a young girl remembering the old man. He is dark and wrinkled with deep eyes. He walks on the mountain, praying. The mountain is said to be the place where Coyote created the world. Coyote pulled the land up out of the fog with a hooked stick.

In a tiny valley with a little spring that creeps across mossy stones, there stands a gnarled, old oak tree, the branches spread down as if to embrace the ground. Woodpeckers softly call and in the brush quail mix into their conversations. The old man sits with his back to the tree, his eyes closed. I had seen him before. Like a yearling colt, ears pricked forward, I awkwardly walk up and say, "Hey." Slowly he looks up, opens his eyes and greets me, "Hello. How are you?" "Fine, but I had some problems getting across Jones's land again." The old man's eyes glint happily. "Oh? The old cowman with the fierce dogs and loose bull?" He seems to be waiting. "Yeah, that's the one," I tell him. "I had to cross his property! In order to get to my favorite places I have to trespass!"

The old man laughs when I tell him this, then says, "In the olden days, the people could become invisible." He grins and gets up, brush-

ing off the oak leaves. He stumps off with a single, backwards, lingering look. My memory vanishes and I am back in the Jeep, thunder from the river loud in my ears. *Old man,* I ask, *How does a person become invisible these days?*

Turning a corner of the road there is a green Suburban truck parked with a man standing near it. He is looking across the river. I slow down and pull up next to him. He turns and smiles through his wet yellow beard. I roll down my window and gasp as the rain whips at my face. My voice shouts, "Have you seen a loose dog?" The man steps closer to my window. He wears a wrinkled greenish uniform and

an old slicker. His hair whips around in the wind like living things about to jump off his head. He leans into the window. Peter growls. The man shouts back, "What did you say?"

My voice rises, "I said, have you seen a dog? I lost a dog." I didn't expect anyone to have seen Mckenzie, she is so shy and hides from people. It is her fear of people that gives her a good chance. But with the storm raging, it is possible that in the confusion she had let herself be seen. Maybe there are tracks. It is easy to tell wolf tracks from dog tracks. (Wolves' outer toes have a gentle curve like a tadpole, whereas dogs' prints have a round or oval shape on both sides of the paw.)

The man leans in closer. "A dog? What does she look like ?" A little shivery signal goes on in my mind like the horse who jumps when a branch falls. "She looks like a sled dog. Light gray, skinny." The man says nothing. Just looks at me. "Who are you?" I ask him.

"Department of Wildlife. I'm a biologist."

Calm, I tell myself as my heart leaps around. Then I say, "Oh yeah, that's interesting. What do you study?" The man pauses, then shouts between gusts, "Grizzly… mostly, but…wolf as well." *Oh, great,* I think to myself, then ask the ranger,

"You seen any?"

He smiles, "Grizzly or wolf?"

"Either?"

"Ah! No! Not really. Where you headed?"

"Up country. Got to find my dog."

The man frowns, reaches up and wipes the rain from his face. "Can't let you do that. The road is blocked up there anyway. The river is flooding!" He waves his hand at the swollen waters running down the mountain beside the road. His slicker blows fiercely in the next gust of wind. I ask myself, *What can they do?* He answers my thought, "State troopers and mounties up there." "Oh," I say, "I'll just turn around and go back. Good bye!" I shout, then add, "What's your name anyway?" He draws a breath and shouts, "Frank, Frank Johnson! What's yours?" I laugh. "Teresa!" His voice rises even higher as the wind catches his next question. "You Native?" I feel the ancestors smiling in the landscape of my mind, in the grassland. Confidently, I answer, "Yes! I'm Native, mixed blood!"

In the summer country, the old man on the mountain smiles at me from another time where the rain is not falling. He walks away from a much younger me. "Yes," he says, "The old people could become invisible."

Chapter Nine

Invisible

Perhaps my blood sees that the old man still stands under the oak. He speaks to the child who had once been me. Grandmother made this place. It is alive! Grandfather made this place and it is alive! See each rock and tree. They are people. I give them some of my hair, a small gift to say, "Thank you! for making such a good place." The old man pulls out a few of his hairs, gray and thick, and lays them at the roots of the oak tree. It had seemed strange to me then. But years later, I begin to understand. The old man gave the tree a piece of himself and laid it where the tree draws nourishment from the earth. He respected the tree as an individual, another being that carries the Life Force.

I watched the wolves become people, I saw that they, too, are caught in the web of life. Wolves and other animals have their own tribes, independant of humans. They are living their lives as best they can, deserving of my respect for their individuality and choice of path in this world. In time, the wolves led me to the others in the world who speak with no words and teach with no books.

Rain drums on the windshield, calling me back into the moment and out of my memories. I need protection. Softly, I say, *Help me find her*. Then thinking of the state troopers and the mounties, I add, *Let me be invisible*. I laugh, it is an odd thing to expect to happen.

Down the road a small turnoff is inviting. It leads to a rough opening back in the brush. Mckenzie is many miles away. On foot, no one would catch me. I park, and then I let Peter and Beanie out. They are glad to be able to stretch. Slinging up my pack, I head into the deepest brush, walking like the deer walk. Step...pause...step...breathe...listen...step.

Habits from hunting with the young wolf are instilled in my body. Gently bend the branches back, step around. Crouch almost double, duck under, watch. Stillness is for listening. The misty earth is fragrant. I caress wet leaves and humus as my hands lightly touch for balance. A twig pokes me showing the openings. With the wind and rain it is unlikely that anyone will hear.

Peter moves ahead, Beanie stays close to me. Carefully I creep to the place where I presume Frank is. Quietly I bark like an angry squirrel to bring Peter and Beanie up close. Peering through deep brush I can barely make out the figure of Frank. He is standing by the truck, possibly fiddling with a camera.

We turn and walk on. The tall evergreen branches heave in the thick canopy above. Their creaks and groans are voices of warning. We have to avoid the road block. After about an hour we reach the top of a rise by an old familiar fire trail. I had walked Mckenzie past here on our way to her release spot, which is still miles away. I wonder if Mckenzie would wander back if she were in trouble. The mud is slick under

my boots. Rain falls in blinding sheets and like a thick membrane covers everything. The wind cries through the trees that bend in submission. The river is the loudest, a rousing sound like the sea.

Peter jogs ahead, his nose to the ground, tasting air like water. Beanie hangs close, nervous. We are planets circling in a solar system of rain. My gear is getting damp. Somewhere the sun blazes in the sky above. Here, the gray deepens. My legs begin to ache. Scars on my body thick and sharp, stand and rattle here and there. My old injuries like crusty, callused friends chat about pride and strength. Ignoring them, I follow Peter's black-tipped tail into the wind.

Suddenly, Peter stops. Time slows until my uneven breath hangs in front of my face, a slowly swirling mist in the sudden calm. Peter turns and stares at me. In those moments, a conversation ensues that has no words, only blood ties to life. Peter tells me, *The mountain is sliding*. All the hairs on Peter's back lift, like an army of spears. There is perfect silence for a moment, then something great breathes beneath our feet.

We both turn and run. The ground shakes like a big animal getting to its feet. Boulders as big as cars crash down. They thunder like charging buffalo. Mud and scree fall with a rasping, silvery sound. The ground throbs under our legs. The roar is deafening. The greatest fear I have ever felt clutches at my chest like a desperate animal.

We run as far as survival, as far as drawing breath. When we stop I look for Beanie and she is there, trembling, by my side. Peter comes to me and licks my hands. I take hold of his big fur ruff and gently shake his head. He responds, as always, by gently growling. Not everything speaks with a voice. Some talk with the language of the body, with a nuance and perception that cannot lie. Horses taught me about the talk that runs in muscle and skin. Peter taught me the language of spirit. I owe Peter my life.

We wait, my body shivering from exhaustion and the electricity of survival. Then cautiously we walk back up the road. My legs start shaking on their own as if they are ready to flee at once. Cautiously approaching the slide, I quickly glance around. We are wild now. Our perceptions tuned and searching. These few steps, like walking towards the persona of death, are the hardest I have ever taken. The mountain is quiet. The river still thunders, the rain flies down in our faces, my slicker flaps in the wind. The road is gone. In its place stands mud, rocks, and boulders. Looking up, I can see a huge gash cut out of the mountainside. The landslide lies in our path.

Shakily walking up to the largest boulder, I pull out some strands of my long dark hair as I had seen the old man himself do long ago. I lay them on the boulder slick with mud and say, *Thank you for my life. Thanks for warning Peter. We're good people. I'm only looking for my little daughter, a gray wolf. Help us find her. Here is my gift.*

The boulder, fresh from the mountain, lies mute in the road, wet and dark. But I feel better. Maybe as the old man had said, something heard our plea for safety. Perhaps the mountains will hold themselves till we have found her, if Mckenzie is still alive. Gingerly we climb over the slide, mud covers my boots and stains Peter's white belly. Panting, we soon stand on the other side. A glance back, I see the towering cliff, its earth smell like a strong broth.

We are on the fire road again and continue as before. With a howl I call Mckenzie. I had spent long hours practicing these drawn-out quavers of song. Peter stops and answers me, sending his ringing voice into the mountains for the young wolf. But the only answer is the wind, and she brings me no news. Peter drinks down great gulps of air. What is the wind saying? What pictures of thought come to Peter?

We turn off the road at the beginning of the little path that leads higher into the mountains, staying close to the trail above the churning river. Numerous, overflowing creeks run down the sides of the mountain to the river coursing rapidly through the narrow ravines. The first one we cross has a convenient old bridge someone made years ago. It is crudely built out of split logs and stuck into the banks. The last time I was here, the creek was far below the slender bridge. But now the rising water foams and tears at the weakening structure. Peter looks at me, his whine scarcely heard. He trots across the bridge, tail held out, nose to the logs. He follows his senses to the bank. Beanie and I follow him.

How many miles now? It has been four hours. Darkness veils the forest. The river becomes a white noise, almost a silence. I slip once and lie in the mud, almost not caring that I had fallen. It is so good to be still. In the warm, calm place deep inside me, I think, *I'll never find her. She's dead in the land-slides. Caught in the flood.* Lying in the dark mud of the trail, hands spread out on the earth, my fingers move convulsively and softness curls up around them. Breathing heavily my thoughts fill the dark. This is where I came from. The black mud. I take from the land to survive and I will give my body back to her when I die. The debt to the land. Do we think we own her? She owns us.

The grass beside the trail pokes my fingers. Dead grass. It will come back in the spring. All life holds hands around the great circle. The water strider gave away to the mallard who gave away to the bobcat who gave away to the grass people who gave away to the deer who gave away to the flies who gave away to the frog who ate the strider. The litany sung by all.

There is balance. Not the stability of the bubble in the carpenter's level but the waning and waxing of the moon. A woman's equilibrium. Balance brings ease like a horse turning

on good footing. Sorry, but death helps twirl the wheel. Look close, the wheel runs in a circle bringing life. Living long in the library makes you nearsighted. Many times it is better to read the trees. The aphids and barnacles, all the numerous, small living things give us bedrock to stand on and from that base we reach, like children, for wisdom. A pity to waste their gift. The little cells that lived in the early seas came together and decided to form the beginnings of body. Cells, small and expandable, form the hands and cradle the spirit. Little watery puffs that later became more complex. Long ago that was me. Does this process ever end? Will I join others and become a larger body, a universal embryo? Or have I already done so?

Peter comes to me and licks my face. I slowly get up and walk on, the mud drips from my hands. We come to the second creek. It leaps on the path like a fierce young horse, bucking and rearing down the mountain to the river now far below. Without a backward glance, Peter runs at the creek and jumps. He sails right across, and turns to look at us. He then trots on.

Beanie sits down while I measure the creek like a rider measuring the distance to a fence. The water is cold, deep enough to sweep me off my feet. How strong is it? How much energy do I have left? I can't wade across. Mckenzie is in that direction. I back up, take off my pack and thrust it under some heavy brush. For a few seconds, I stare at the rushing water, while the rain runs off my hat brim. Then, I run at the creek and jump, arms outstretched towards the opposite bank. Falling half in, half out of the foaming water, cold stings my legs. My hands tear at the icey-cold rocks of the bank. The water drags on me, threatening to rip away my grasp. I cling and struggle, pulling myself out. Beanie crouches by the creek, unwilling to jump, and knows that swimming is impossible. If she tries she will be carried down the mountainside to the river. I yell at her to stay.

Exhausted and wet, I wonder, *Should we stop, make shelter, and start a fire?* The darkness surrounds me, making the storm seem even more ominous. Peter howls a piercing throaty sound standing out like a knife above the wind. In the distance, there is the rumbling roar of another landslide slipping down wet mountains. Fearfully, I look up and plead with the mountain-sides, *Let me find her. Hold yourselves till then. I don't care afterwards, I'll be so happy.*

The little path beckons up the mountain and I follow. Beanie waits by the last creek. It is hard to leave her there but if there is no sign of Mckenzie, I will go back. Peter gives his short, "Buff! Buff!" sound in the distance. His voice pulls me in that direction. On the path I call Mckenzie's name, which the wind takes and chases away. The dark trees toss old needles and small branches spray me.

In the distance, something moves, then another dark shape jumps in the thick woods. The rain has painted the hair down on my face, making it difficult to see into the gloom. I squint my eyes, peer long into what could be a dream. There...in the distance...are the forms of two running wolves. Peter bounces happily with Mckenzie. They fly at me with great bounding leaps, and when they reach me they swarm, clawing and licking. My face becomes hot and tears mingle with wolf fur. Mckenzie nips my face as little whistling sounds escape from her mouth in between licking and pinching me. My cold hands rub her warm body in the dark. She is thinner, but unharmed and tighter somehow. Peter brushes his head under my hand. "Thanks Pete for finding her." By smell or perception Peter knew where Mckenzie was. It also seems like Mckenzie had come to find us. For whatever reason, Mckenzie had called me to her in the wilderness and now she needs to return with me for a while longer. It is not yet time for the final release.

After a few exhilarating minutes of reunion, I stand up, wiping the tears and rain from my face. I realize that we must get out. We might not get back if we do not leave immediately. But my legs are stiff and I move slowly.

When my father died my step-grandmother told me, "Your grief is big because your love is big." Grief, like water, rushes in to fill the hole that carried love. And in time you may have a lake that the water birds migrate to. That hole is also like death. Fear of falling keeps us clinging to the edge, holding tufts of grass. But if you jump you might splash into the warm water of a tropical sea. There in the rain on the mountain I know my heart holds the joy of this moment and the grieving lake. Some day Mckenzie will be free. And I will be without her. But for now, we turn and walk back together.

Beanie waits for us at the last creek. This time Peter and Mckenzie wait for me to jump first. They nose around the brush, peering at the water, breathing quickly. It is now dark. Where is the narrow place? Pacing, my thoughts leap happily around the fact that I have Mckenzie back. We have luck and that gives me flight. Rushing at the creek and jumping, my knees slap down in the mud of the bank. It is a good leap and

Mckenzie (top) and Peter.

carries me further than before. I am still wet, but the wool under my slicker is warm.

Peter and Mckenzie jump easily. Beanie wags her tail furiously and licks my hands, forgiving me for leaving her. Searching for a moment through the underbrush in the dark I pull out my pack. The damp earth smells pleasant and comforting. I sling the pack up on my shoulders and we continue to walk.

Soon we get to the second creek. Raging now, water tugs at the log bridge I can hardly see. The wolves wait casually in the woods on either side of the path. Two wolf stars in the forest night, trees surround their bright spirits. They are calm. I focus on the other side of the creek and start walking carefully across. Under my feet the water rings with power, sucking at the log bridge. It trembles like something very old. Once across, I look back. We have found the Gray One. Now we have to make it back. Beanie follows right behind me. Peter and Mckenzie pay no attention to the water flowing rapidly under their noses. They trot across the bridge with balanced self-assurance.

My eyes can see much better at night because of the months of hunting deer in the dark with Mckenzie. But I am weary from this journey and I decide to risk walking down the little fire road to the regular road. Better to face the state troopers than walk over a ridge and fall. Mckenzie will hide if we see anyone.

How long has it been since I had talked with Frank? Six hours? Eight? We walk along in the dark. We hear another avalanche in the distance. All of us stop. My breath hides in my chest. We pause like Deer Woman, like the Wolf People. We have learned their silence and listen with all their senses to feel through the body where to go and how to get there. Wind and rain surround us. Are the mountains waiting?

Standing a moment and listening, the river thunderously plunges down the mountainsides. The booming shakes the air.

We walk down and come to where the avalanche blocks the road. The ground's uneasiness spreads up through my legs. The earth warning, the blessing of Earth, the mother who watches over all lost children. I hold my hands out low over the unsteady land, and mutter my fear to her: *Let us get back now, we've come so far. We are living something that is important. We are learning something. You have never had far to reach to take my life. Let us get back.* We climb carefully over the boulders and the broken ground.

Scrambling to the other side of the torn-out spill of rock and mud, a sudden stirring of living blood rushes through veins that fills us all. Jumping and yelling, we tumble madly down the slope. Mckenzie frisks, pulling at my coat with her teeth, telling me suddenly of her adventures. My hands sink deep in her warm fur as she jumps, licking at my mouth. Then she steals the glove off my hand and runs around with it, tail kinked, eyes mad with devilment and happiness. We walk on, Mckenzie carries my glove.

Up ahead, Peter stops again. There is a dark shape on the road. The clouds break apart and an elk bull stands watching us. Then he turns with a start, lays back his head, and crashes through the brush, also trying to escape the flood. I call Peter to me and I am surprised that Mckenzie does not follow the elk. She is smarter now. She knows who to hunt and how to ask. The bull is not here to give-away. Mckenzie knows it would take more than just her to pull him down. My boots are damp and squeak as we hike. Are the troopers still on the road?

Down and down. Delicious, the Jeep's heater seems to me

now. How good it will feel to be out of the dripping rain. I have hardly eaten or slept for two days. The distance we have traveled seems incredible. Peter woofs softly, what does he see? In the dark I can make out a round shape, too close. There are a few grumbling groans that tumble down to us, worried sounding. It is a bear. Life tells us to stay still. The bear starts running up the slope to our right. Peter's hair stands up. Grabbing his collar, I say, "Peter, you can't chase that bear, she will turn and come after you! Then we'll be a sight, running across the roadblock with Bear chasing us. The ranger will not let us through then." Peter allows me to restrain him. I peer into the darkness, vaguely sensing the bear stop to take one more look before heading into the brush. My breath comes easier after Bear leaves. A confused bear with the wolves would be hazardous. Mckenzie had hidden at the first sight of the bear, but now comes out. The Gray One is wild. She is going back.

Traveling with Mckenzie, we move down more than this fire road. There is a life trail we walk that we cannot turn around on. She has killed and she has been free. Will she go back to live wild, or will she die in the attempt? Or will she choose to stay with me? Watching at her play in the dark with my glove, I silently promise her that she will choose. Mckenzie is a person deserving respect, she has that right. Sighing to myself, missing her already, I know that she will decide as all people do. But she is with me now, her graceful, gray body and amber eyes.

Years from now I know I will remember this over and over. Her soft fur and the cold rain. The moment belongs to infinity. When I am older I will still hold these moments with every breath and heart beat. In my memory Mckenzie always

walks and hunts no matter what. A child's voice says over and over, *We will do this! We will be free.*

We come to the paved road and walk on that for a while. The rain and wind diminish. Something looms up ahead. It looks like a large fence. The yellow-and-black barrier stands across my path. Sandbagged, formidable, the road block's color is dimmed by the dark. I stop, but there is no one here. No troopers, no mounties. I clamber through but the wolves

Photo: Sylvia Martino

Teresa with Mckenzie, Peter, and Beanie.

scramble with greater dignity. Beanie crouches under awkwardly, and looks at me reproachfully. She has had enough fuss for these wolves! Beanie has never understood my involvement with them.

We are in the brush long before we get to the spot where I had met Frank. It is hard to tell in the dark but I feel in the gathering silence that the road has long since been deserted. And then, I spot Cherry. My legs start shaking from fatigue

and the pain from landing on my knees. The wolves and Beanie are excited. They happily jump up on the doors of the Jeep, leaving great big muddy paw marks. Opening the door, they jump eagerly inside.

The sturdy little engine jumps to life and when the heat comes on full blast, we sit in comfort. My legs and feet begin to tingle pinpricks as the warmth soaks into my body. Drowsy, my eyes close for a moment, then a sharp fear pulls me back with a start. The water! The river is rising, we have to leave now.

When we start down the road, the rain and wind have dwindled. But, the river still roars like an avalanche in the slender silence the weather allows. A turn in the road and I slam on the brakes. The Jeep slides to a stop as I peer through the window in amazement at the scene before us. The road is gone. In its place swirls the muddy water heading for the sea. The river has flung out an arm on the outside of a natural bend. The water covers the road. How deep? Like the river of my childhood, the water spreads out carrying debris. The man in green appears in my mind. If anyone finds us, they might take Mckenzie from me. They will cage her for life, far from her family. I have to get back home with no chance meetings.

Beanie and Peter and Mckenzie are all sound asleep, curled up in the warmth together, trusting me. Pop swims into my thoughts. He is not here to stand before the flood water, but he has taught me. Getting out of my Jeep, I study the swirls, eddies, and riffles. What are they trying to say? Pop was fishing, the fly line gracefully licking the air. He said, "Sister, look at the river, the surface will tell you what is hidden." Then the old man joined Pop in my mind, laying his hair at the base of the old oak on the mountain in the summer country.

Stepping up close to the river, I watch the ripples a little longer to gauge the current's path. The muddy water touches the tips of my boots as I lean close to the water. My hands twine around a few strands of hair, I pull them and then place them in the dark water. They swirl on the surface. I turn back to the Jeep and unlock my hubs to free the wheels. Getting back in the Jeep, I angle my wheels. The river will push me towards the bank downstream, the way I would go if swimming.

Cherry is in four-wheel drive as we start out from the bank. The water gets deep quickly and starts to come in under the doors. Is it going to rise high enough that it chokes the engine to silence? The water rises and sickeningly there is a lightness in the rear tires. Is the Jeep going to get turned around? Rolled over? I may have to swim out. But how will I get the wolves and Beanie out if we are submerged? Am I half-way across? Slowly, the Jeep moves forward as the moon breaks through the clouds and turns the water silver. And in the next moment I can tell the water is shallower! We are almost there! We make it to the other side. For a moment, I look back at the water surging over the road, the blood of the land shines in the moonlight.

Once again on solid ground, the Jeep edges away from the hungry water. There is no one on the mountain roads. The rain has stopped. About three hours later we reach the first town and I park at a small barbecue place. I lie down with the wolves and dog and sleep. Exhaustion takes over every other need.

The next day we drive nonstop, reaching the ferry at dusk. In the evening light the little island looks as if it had never known a storm. At the cabin, the wolves relax in their wolf pen and I sit, my legs weak and cramping, my body unwinding. My eye catches the flickering of the answering machine light, one of my few modern conveniences. I push the red button, and a voice says, "Hello, Ms. Martino? This is Frank Johnson. We found your Jeep but couldn't find you.

We are starting to get together a search party. If you get home please call us." Then another message with a different voice comes on, "Yes, this is Officer Madlen. Would you please call the state troopers' office." Oh God! Slumping down to sit on the floor, I struggle to pull off my boots because the laces are tight and wet, and hard to untie. *Why be afraid?* I ask myself. *It's okay. I'll just tell them I'm safe.*

First, I call the troopers. They are casual after hearing I am home. They had taken down my license plate number. I thank them for their concern. Then I call Frank. He answers smoothly.

"Hello?"

"Yes, it's me, Teresa."

"Oh! I'm glad you called! Are you okay?"

"Yeah, fine."

"Did you find your dog?"

"Uh, yeah, I did."

"Good. What does she look like again?"

Mckenzie comes in through her wolf door and lies by the stove where there is a little rug, her bed. I look at her softly. "Well, like a gray husky." "Gray, huh?" "Yeah. Hey, thanks for trying to help." "No problem. Look, I'm going to send you some pictures I took. They're distant, but it might be your dog." He hesitates, and then adds, "Or it might be a wolf."

"A wolf!" I try to sound surprised but my heart sinks down in my chest like a clam in deep sand. "Yes, I want you to tell me if this is your dog. Can you do that?" "Oh sure," I answer wondering if I could I rip up those pictures when they come. "Great! I got your address from the troopers. Glad you are okay! Hey, don't do anything like that again. Are you nuts or what? You could have been killed!" "I'll look at the pictures," I say and hang up. Mckenzie raises her sleepy face, her golden eyes slits in the white fur. She looks knowingly at me.

Two days later the pictures arrive. It is Mckenzie taken at a great distance, blurred, but unmistakably her. The old man on the mountain, in the little valley where the old oak stands, walking away, turns and looks at me, speaking quietly into my memory.

Invisible.

Chapter Ten

The Guide and the Guardian

"Grandpa?"

"Yeah?" Grandpa is sitting at the yellow kitchen table staring out at the garden where Granny once grew vegetables. The black dirt is turned but empty. "Do you remember the story about the Osage coming from the sky?" "Tres, I wish you'd forget about all of that." He pushes a cup of tea my way. And Margaret, my step-grandmother, sits down next to us.

"Grandpa, how can we forget? If we forget then it's over." Grandpa sighs, "My mother would have said it was dangerous and foolish." I persist, wanting answers. "What would *her* mother have said?" "Well, now..." Grandpa turns his head and looks out of the little window. "You know your book, *Learning from Eagle*...? This is my favorite poem." Grandpa picks up the book and flips to the second to last page. He reads:

There is a void,
a breaking of the circle,
a bundle of sage tossed away.

I see the great grassland,
my relatives crying
don't forget us,
don't forget us,
we're part of you.
My grandpa's family didn't speak of it.
Their stories are buried with their dead.
Their skills sleep in the past.
They were told to be ashamed,
to hide from themselves.
But as Grandfather has told me
everything seeks balance.
Their blood now sings in my body.
It is awake and it teaches me.

As the sun walks backwards,
one of my relatives raised his bow
in anger and sadness.
His arrow flew and now here in the north,
I catch it.

Grandpa turns to face me, his black eyes sharp and mysterious, he does not say anything else but his eyes tell me. Grandpa was taught not to talk about this as a young boy. My eyes answer. Amber-brown wolf eyes answer the silence that has followed my family for one hundred years. My eyes say, *I'm proud of you Grandpa. I'm proud of my blood. Ancestors! Have I done right by you?* I feel them say, *Don't forget us!* Grandpa smiles slightly, and puts down the book.

"Mom?" I hold the phone close to my ear, dark hair pushed back out of the way. It is morning and the cabin is filled with light. It is important for me to tell the people whom I love where I am going. "Yes?" "I'm going to the

mountains. I've circled on a map where I'll be if you need me. I'll leave it in the cabin." I can see Mom sitting on the tall stool by the sliding-glass door. The same place she sat when the hospital called to tell us Pop was dead. For some reason I remember how she looked getting that news. She slid down gently till her head and arm rested lightly on the counter top. I knew what was wrong without hearing. Now, Mom's face is tired and worried. Her hair is iron dark in back and is the color of cinnamon in front with gray blend-

ing with the rest. She looks at me through the phone wires. I feel her wild-horse stare, the whites of her eyes glittering. "Be careful...I'll pray for you." "Mom, I'm taking the gift you saw me paint. I'm giving it to the deer." Her eyes spark and jump. "Be careful."

These days spin around me as winter's end slowly turns to spring. It is the time of "without warning" storms and bitter March winds. I do not think too much, only act like the wolf or the horse, my teachers. If I think too much I may lose my resolve. You are hungry you hunt. If you are thirsty find water. One more phone call to make....There is snow on the ground outside and it blows through the thin cabin walls.

"Mike?" The phone receiver is cold and I rub my free hand on my pants. "Yes, T." Phones are lonely things and I wish I could look Mike in the face and ask him this with my heart in my eyes. The wind finds a crack and jabs my knee with an icy touch. "I have a favor to ask you. I need you to come to the mountains with Mckenzie and me. We're going on our last hunt. You can watch for us and keep people away."

In my mind, I see Mike turning his big shaggy head full of long red hair and beard. I see him brush his hands across his wilderness ranger uniform. He works for the United States Forest Service, or "circus" as Mike puts it. If he helps me he will risk his job if we are caught. But someone has to keep people away from us and sadly, to scare Mckenzie into not following me back. "Of course," Mike says. "When?"

The winter is finally dead and a surge of energy is flooding our bodies. The tiny buds we thought were imagined lift their way out of the branches to scratch at the sky. Soon the deer will have their young. Mckenzie needs to be released in the spring while there will be young animals to catch.

Mckenzie is nearly a year old and well fed. She weighs more than one hundred pounds. If her paws are on my shoulders, her nose is above my five-foot-five-inch body. When she runs and spreads her feet out, her paw print is as big as my hand. It is her grace that moves me. She trots with such floating strides and turns and stares with eyes like a bird of prey. Tall and long legged, her overcoat is coming out in draggled patches. But her mane and ruff are fully four inches long and flecked with black. Several Native people told me that young female wolves are the best hunters

because they are quick. Mckenzie is strong. She is ready. We have to go soon.

I plan our leaving date. Kip's release was a soft gentle introduction. He literally melted back into the wild, like rain falling to the ground, quickly absorbed into the earth. Perhaps Mckenzie will find her home in the wilderness with the same ease.

Mike must take his own truck. Mckenzie will not tolerate him riding in the Jeep. I pack as lightly as possible. My gear includes boots, two pairs of wool and silk socks, long underwear, wool shirts, a coat, my long riding duster of waxed cotton, and my waxed cotton hat, rumpled and chewed, but warm and dry. I also bring fire starter wrapped tightly in plastic along with matches and wood chips. At Mike's insistence I bring green plastic garbage bags. He loves plastic garbage bags. He claims that you can do anything with them—-build a shelter, use them for rain gear. Mike makes a rustling noise when he walks, a "shish, shish" from the sound of the plastic. Mike also has a lot of gear made from the new materials invented for mountain climbing. I prefer wool and silk.

We plan a minimum amount of fires so as not to attract attention. When possible, we will travel at night, at dawn, and at dusk, and try to sleep during the day. Mckenzie needs to get a deer while we are there. But I include dog food to cache, which she hates. I must know that Mckenzie can hunt deer. This will reassure me that she can make it on her own. Constantly I ask myself, *Am I releasing her just to die?*

When the time comes to go, I find myself in that same uneasy place that I feel when I run horses. The moment that is bigger than drawing breath and lasts forever, and there I am—immortal. There is a furious gaiety in the world, a running elk lightness. There is a knowing that is as intoxicating as whiskey, spinning my mind. I love the chase. This is why I jump horses. I am trying to remove the halter from my own neck, but do I place it on others? I ride without equipment and my horses carry me willingly. Perhaps in my poverty they lend me their freedom to teach me. And Mckenzie is giving me the same gift.

The Jeep is packed and Mckenzie gets in, thinking we will both return. How can she not think that? We belong to each other, we are like a pack. The young wolf thinks that life will be what it has always been, that I will always be with her. I cannot tell her. She does not realize what my intentions are. For that, Gray One, I beg your forgiveness.

On the way to the ferry Mckenzie sleeps, trustingly, in the back. The drive is empty. Mckenzie may not be returning. Most likely she will never see the cabin or Peter or Beanie again. The ferry swings up and down on the back of the Sound and I remember Peter's parting look. I sensed that he knew what was going to happen. His wise face had a mournful expression when we left.

Getting off the ferry we drive to the northern mountains where I plan to hike across the border to Canada. The weather is perfect, sunny but cool. It is early spring in the north. We drive the highways of the Pacific Northwest past new construction of malls and restaurants. Is this the halter to tame our own wildness? We have taught ourselves to need so many things when very little is really necessary. Mike's truck follows behind me, his quiet solemn face reassuring in my rearview mirror. Mckenzie is peaceful, hardly pacing at all. She looks out the tinted windows with her intelligent stare, watching the highway rolling ahead of us.

This feels like the hardest thing I have ever done but I have to start this process. Wolves are loyal. She will never part from me on her own. I must be strong for us both.

Damn it! Why is the world like this? Why do I owe it any loyalty? The wolves are my relatives but not my tribe. When I leave Mckenzie in the wild, I will return to the island, to my cabin, and live with humanity. I think of Mckenzie's mother pacing in the small circular prison at the rescue center. I am still struggling against my own chain-link fences, but Mckenzie is wild now. I have asked myself so many times, *Is this what you want for Mckenzie?* No chain link Gray One. Mckenzie is my daughter.

Is this our children's future? To be surrounded by fences that separate us from our world, the wild, and each other? The old man on the mountain told me he thought we kept coming back again and again. He said he believed this because Earth does this too. Everything returns. We will face the problems we leave for our children. We will be them.

After four days of driving we get to the trailhead where we will begin the hike. I am familiar with this area because Mckenzie and I have hunted here. I have seen wolf signs in these woods: a few tracks and scat. Mckenzie needs to leave her scent for that tiny pack so they will be familiar with her. The young wolf will not have her first serious heat until she is two years old, but she is still a desirable member of a pack at one year old. She is large and confident.

We park by some brush and I get out to talk with Mike. "I'll go on ahead with her and then stop when it's time to camp." Mike's expression is soft, "I'll whistle if I see anyone." I go back to the Jeep and let Mckenzie out. She bounds by me and after throwing a fearful glance at Mike, disappears into the foliage. I sling up my pack and start after her. She soon comes out to join me, frisking along with her playful stride. She looks back and sees that Mike is coming too, and she slinks off into the salal. Mike is tall and big shouldered. He looks like a bear as he trudges patiently up the hill. Mckenzie and I move ahead of him.

Afternoon shadows grow as the sun slips towards the snow-covered mountains tinged blue in the changing light. A contrast with the trees and brush touched with the brilliant green of spring. Going into the mountains, sounds of life wrap around what our crazy world calls silence. I hear the soft voices of birds and water. Wind sighs, feathered wings flap, an excited squirrel barks. This is our home these voices tell me. *Here you are with us again*, they say. And it does not matter if you are dirty or poor. All are the same here. All take the same chances.

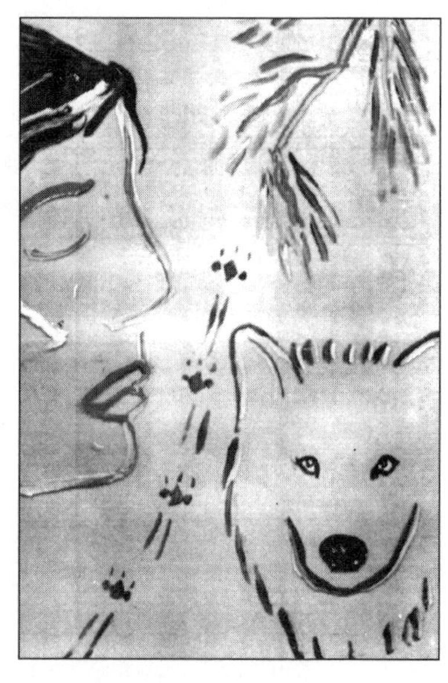

In the beginning of our journey we quiet our thoughts till we begin to move slower and slower, cautious so that we will not be caught. We do not speak as we pass gently through the brush. Mike knows that I do not want to use the main trails, so we follow the bear and the water upstream as much as we can.

Since Mike and I cannot walk together because of Mckenzie's fear, I feel alone in all of this. I watch for deer sign and wonder if this is right. *Can Mckenzie really go back? She has hunted and killed*, I repeatedly tell myself. But only small game. Can she kill a deer? By herself? Deer are hardy

animals and can fight with their sharp hooves and antlers very effectively. The old woman from the rescue center told me that she had almost been killed by an elk bull who had no antlers at the time. Pop had seen a doe kill a snake.

Mckenzie will certainly find the other wolves but will they accept her? The voice of one of the wildlife officials I had talked with in the past comes to mind. "The other wolves will kill her, a stranger on their territory." But not all animals act the same. They are all as different as we are.

Was this an acceptable risk? Mckenzie would choose this life rather than be penned up forever. And what about me? What would I do now that I have been free? What is freedom? It lies in the mouth of the wolf bringing food to the pack. And it is tucked under the wings of the monarch butterfly returning home to the warm shores of the summer country. After I have been out this far can I really ever go back?

That night Mike makes a small fire at our campsite and cooks soup. Mckenzie disappears and my heart sinks knowing that she will not sleep next to me because of Mike's presence. I get out one of my favorite shirts, which is wrapped around a special object, my gift. It is painted with a hawk, a tree, a wolf, and a deer. I pray with it in my hands. I pray that the deer will be generous to the young wolf.

Mike and I talk softly in our brush voices of things that people have wondered about. The night woods bring out these feelings. Amidst our talk there is a gentle noise, starting high and thin, a frail spider web of a call. It is the graceful voice of Mckenzie throwing her soul at the sky. She tells me she is lonely. She asks why am I with this stranger and not with her? Then silence. Several heartbeats later in the distance the faint answering cry of another wolf. If the stranger had not answered McKenzie, my heart would have broken and I would still hear her trembling cry of sorrow. In that moment I remember my dream, walking with Mckenzie through snow-covered mountains searching for something. The journey is right. This is the correct path.

Sleeping on the soft earth I wander the woods with the Gray One in my dreams. When we wake it is still dark and we quickly pack up and head out. I go ahead so Mckenzie will walk with me. She soon pops out of the brush and greets me by running up bowing, front legs splayed. Then she leaps up, licks and nips at my mouth. Following the creeks we head for the northernmost edge of the western states. There are national and provincial parks that straddle the border and I hope Mckenzie will find safety there. In these parks no hunting is permitted.

As we walk we slip between time. The moments slow down until they become a bubble of fresh water on the edge of a river. The idea of forever is guarded not by hard walls but by a thin film that, when it pops, you will spill out and mix with eternity. Human beings have walked like this, pacing along in partnership with the wolf and woods, only their small belongings with them. If they were tired, they sat and rested. Hungry, they stopped and ate. They looked for game, smell the air. The metal smell meant water was close by. Listen! Is it Bear Woman or Elk Man? There must be a balance between wild and tame, between partnership and bondage. There must be new words created to better explain the wild, and to better understand our civilization. The wilderness has laws, very strict ones.

We come across a large Douglas fir. On this tree are scratches made deep in the bark, six feet over my head. There are a few thick brownish hairs stuck on the bark. I wait for Mike. We look at one another, no words needed. Here is the chief of the woods. The one who we tiptoe around. We begin to trace the wind's path and walk with the breeze blowing up

from behind us so that Bear will know we are here. Bear is the one who taught humanity what to eat. Bear is the one who shows us that there is spring after the dark of winter. My friend, Curly, has said, "Know how not to get eaten by Bear? Don't go where she is!"

Once at a party a young man exclaimed to me, shocked, "You don't carry a gun?" I told him, "No, I carry no weapons. I carry my eyes and ears and the ability to be silent. And I don't walk in the wilderness like I am master, but rather like a child of the land, subject to her rules." The world knows if you carry fear.

During the day Mike and I decide to keep hiking to get as far up and out as we can. Time has stopped but the moment holds and the days blend together sweetly. The weather is still clear and the sun hints of warmth. I write poems and stuff them in my pockets, hoping they will make it back somehow. Sometimes I do not think I will ever come back.

I walk toward the mountains
gray, dark dawn mountains
sided with shadows,
wearing snow on their tops.

Gray One followed
trotting, trotting,
through the trail.

Far away I could hear singing,
the singing of the wolf people,
calling the Gray One.

One afternoon we camped and sat in the brush. And at some point I looked at Mike and said, "Do you hear that?"

"Yes," he whispered. "What is it?" "I'm not sure." The sound came from all directions. It had a pleasing musical tone to it rather like chimes or little tinkling bells. Millions of them chimed together, close but not too loud. We listened for hours. We never figured out what they were. Finally, at dusk, we got up and walked on.

We make camp near a high mountain lake that in the distance sounds like a big animal crashing through the brush. So I secretly name the lake "Sounds Like a Bear." Mike is bear-like too, all hunched over under his enormous pack. I feel light, like antelope.

In the morning, Mckenzie disappears for a while. When she returns she is dragging the silken liner of an expensive sleeping bag. Mike and I look at one another and laugh. "Someone is going to have a good story." Mike rubs his beard and holds up an invisible phone: "Hello, park department, I want to report my sleeping bag was stolen in one of your parks by a wolf." Mckenzie frisks gaily about with her prize, galloping madly by, enticing me to chase her. I hope she has not let the poor people see her.

We start again and follow a narrow deer trail. In the distance we hear voices. Mike and I step into the brush, melt down, and listen. Two voices talk loudly about home and work. They march up the trail where the pale elk steps like a ghost. Mckenzie has gone that way. Soon, quite clearly, I hear the woman gasp,

"God! It's a wolf!

Look! It's a wolf."

"It can't be!" says the man, "let me see! My God, it is a wolf! I can't believe it. I saw a bear once and now a wolf!"

"Are you sure? Maybe it's a big coyote?"

"A coyote as big as a pony?"

"Well, it's gone now."

"Yeah, maybe we should report it."

There is a pause, then an afterthought jumps in. "Honey, do you have both sleeping bag liners? I couldn't find mine."

The voices get louder and louder as they hike down the trail. Soon they are right next to us. Hidden and still, we watch them. I feel bad for the hikers. I want to rush out and tell them my story. "Look folks, this is the way it is." But I don't. I am always struck at how many mysteries surround us without us seeing them. For the brief moment these people sighted a wild wolf, they nearly sighted wild people.

The hikers head down the trail towards the ranger station with their wolf news. A day later we hear the howling of park rangers. Walking up the trail on foot, they stop and howl. Hidden in the bush, I listen. Mckenzie is curled up beside me. She does not even raise her head when the rangers howl. I do not know whether to laugh or send my own call ringing back to them.

What would happen if I answer and then, with the Gray One, step into their path? Why do I think they would hate my freedom? I do not have a piece of paperwork that gives me permission to know wolves, no degree in biology. But I resent that everything I know or say about wolves will be taken with a grain of salt because I am not college educated or a biologist. I have worked with animals all my life, but scientists would question what I might possibly know about them. While scientists may go and observe a pack of wolves, I *live* with the wolves. This is where science fails us. It does not allow for the individuality of the animals, or the individuality of the family unit or pack. Scientists want to put everything in a box, categorize life. The Mystery gave all living things individuality in order to survive. If we are flexible, we can survive.

The rangers roam up the trail and make camp, blocking our way into the high mountains. We had come so far, but after a long discussion, Mike and I decide we will go back to the vehicles and approach the wilderness from a different trail. If the rangers spot Mckenzie they will not leave her alone. Quickly, we start back down the mountain, retracing our path. I wonder if Mckenzie will get back into the Jeep. She has been hunting throughout the trip and has caught rodents and a bird. When we reach the cars I give Mckenzie a pill to tranquilize her. It is tough to fool her but I had brought some meat for just such an emergency. Rolling the drug into a little ball of meat, I hand it to Mckenzie. She spits it out a couple of times, then swallows it. I carry syringes if I have to tranquilize Mckenzie in an emergency, but I have never had to use one.

After twenty minutes I try to put her into the Jeep. No way. She will not jump in and growls if I try to lift her inside. Finally, after much pulling and frantic wrestling, each of us trying not to hurt the other, I manage to get her in. She is swaying unsteadily and lies down and sleeps. All night I drive towards the border. Mike follows me. When we get close to Canada, I signal to Mike to pull over. In the same thought I

consider the old man of my youth and the ranger, Frank.

"Mike, they are going to search the car at the border." Glancing into the back seat, I add, "They won't be fooled by her." We are standing on the main highway into Canada and a few cars whiz by us blowing my coat and tugging at my braided hair. In my mind I call on the old man, and out loud tell Mike, "We have to pray for protection, for invisibility. It's worked for me before." Mike's eyes rest softly on my face. "Okay."

We drive into Canada, Grandmother's country, and are immediately signaled by the patrol to pull over. We park our cars and go inside the drab beige building to stand in line and state our business and declare our possessions. Then the officers follow us outside to examine our cars. One man opens Mike's rusty truck door, which squeaks in protest as he pulls it open. The officer pushes his hat back with one hand and reaches for the little shoe box filled with syringes and tranquilizer pills.

My eyes catch Mike's. I feel the blood drain from my face. We will be arrested. My heart speeds up and my hands start to shake. I had totally forgotten about the drugs. I pray, *Don't see it! Don't see this.* The officer shakes the box then gently, slowly, sets it down and turns to look inside an extra pair of Mike's shoes. He then shuts the door, smiles into my frightened face, and looks underneath the car. Nothing. Then he walks to my Jeep. Mckenzie is swaying in the back, woozy from the tranquilizer. I pray harder, *Don't see her, don't see her.* The wind stirs the air and my Jeep's antenna blows back and forth with a little vibrational twang. The officer looks into the driver's side and opens the door. Then he peers into the shadows of the back. He had to be staring directly into the golden eyes where the mountains are reflected. Mckenzie never flinches.

The man draws his head back out and turns to us. I am shaking like I never thought I could. So afraid. I have been very close to Bear and never trembled like this. "Okay," the man says slowly, "you can go." He waves us off and in shock we get back into the cars. The wind picks up, sounding like wolves. The sting of rain grazes my cheeks and darkens Mike's beard.

We are invisible.

Chapter Eleven

Daughters of the Wild

The land is lonely for the soft paws of wolves. Mother Earth reaches up with tender hands of mud and dust to embrace our feet to carry us through The Mystery. I always felt that the island loved the young wolf, it had waited such a long time for wolves.

Now, the voice of mountains sings to Mckenzie as we drive the roads. The song rings in our bones and mingles somehow with the radio playing Canadian country music. The Jeep tires leave deep tracks and I wonder if the land remembers us when we leave our prints on her.

Once past the border patrol it seems like a dream, the kind of dream with dark edges around crystal clarity. The eyes of the old man and the red-tailed hawk peer into my mind. We park near some brush and sleep in the cars. I am exhausted. I crave sleep and the sacred place where the spirits talk as I dream. Tonight it is of a woman and a man, a little child, a fawn, a black mare, and a small fox. A white wolf who speaks like a person, says, *You must fast and pray. You are living a story about going back, about how it will be with the wolves and the human beings. The deer are watching to see if you are worthy. Leave them a gift. Be strong and pray.*

We wake in the cool blue twilight time a few hours before dawn. The windows are foggy with our breath. I feel a rush of anxiety urging us, *Go on, immediately!* I pray and from then on I fast.

Getting out of the Jeep, Mckenzie leaps by me, the tranquilizer long since worn off. The wolf runs up the dirt road. Looking back, I see that Mike is getting out of his truck, slinging up his big pack. In front of us are the snow-capped mountains I had seen in my dreams so long ago when the Gray One was a baby. Our plan is to hike back across the border into the United States in order to once again reach the wilderness area that I think will be the best for Mckenzie's release.

Walking quickly up the dirt road there are two little cabins, a flag waves above them—-park headquarters. One cabin has a light on and a figure moves inside putting coffee on the stove. It is a comforting sight for us, so far away from our own homes. I think of breakfast in the morning, waking with the wolves in my cabin, coffee boiling on the wood stove. Those times are gone now and I grieve.

We are invisible. We walk right down the road in full view of the front window. A wolf, a woman, and a man walk towards some of the last wilderness areas in North America. The wolf to go home; the woman to make peace with blood; the man, I do not know why, perhaps to help. That is enough.

We come to a little creek where I kneel and from my pack pull out my gift. So many old precious objects were taken away from the ancestors. I brought a symbol of these old things, sacred and beyond price, that represent a culture forgotten by my family. Now, I give the gift back to the land. I

unwrap and bury the gift in the ground by the creek, then cover the spot with heavy river stones. I ask the deer for the great favor: Life for the Gray One.

Then we walk into the woods and the clouds fall down on us. It grows colder. The thought of hypothermia zigzags across my mind. We stop and Mike gets out his plastic bags to wrap around him. I find a log caught on another tree and begin to lay old branches and to pile leaves against it. I crawl under and my heat is captured by the leaf litter piled up above me. Mike crawls in too. We are both cold from walking too fast and getting sweaty. We soon warm up and I fall asleep to more dreams.

When I wake up in the hut of branches and leaves, I look out. In the mist Mckenzie stands in front of me. My dream was a deep well where I saw the little face of Kip peering at me, his furry tail whipping in a circle. He spoke, *We're all here. We are praying for you.* Mckenzie trots up to me in my dream and I look into her gentle face with the fierce golden eyes. She changes, her paws grow bigger and darker, her claws grow longer. She is enormous. She has become Grizzly. I wake with a start and crawl out of the den under the log. I hear rustling in the brush and then the land becomes still.

The old doe walks slowly like an ancient priestess, and so she is. Heavy with fawn, she paces toward me on her delicate hooves. Am I still dreaming? Looking into my eyes, the doe occasionally bobs her head, and flicks her long ears. She sighs and gently walks toward Mike, sniffing the quiet wind. I stalk a few steps trying to hold her with my gaze and softly call Mckenzie.

The doe is giving-away. The doe looks at the place where, in a moment, Mckenzie will come bursting out. And then the deer melts back into the brush. Mckenzie comes and then follows her. Mike and I rush after them to watch.

The doe gives away as a noble-hearted person gives for the life of a child. She gives herself to Mckenzie and me. Wolf and Doe run across a meadow full of rain and shadow. They run slowly the way constellations turn in the sky, then disappear into the forest.

We can hear the crashing of the doe, the rhythmic sound as she bolts through the brush but we cannot see them. Mckenzie disappears like white mist into the woods and soon we are alone. The land has swallowed them both up into mystery. My hands are clenched at my side, my throat is dry, and I suddenly feel weak. In the stillness, a whiskey jack comes to look closely at us from a low branch. And then the forest breathes. I look at Mike. His eyes and mine speak without voices. It is time to go. Mckenzie will catch the doe, of this I am sure. So while she chases her life that slips from the deer, we will fall out of her world. As I go, tears come and drip on my arms, sliding to the earth where Mckenzie had recently walked by my side.

Mike and I start the long walk back. Several hours later Mckenzie meets me. In her mouth is the leg of the doe. She had followed me and I now know that she will be all right. For years to come I will offer thanks to the old doe.

We sat in the brush
where I knew the Deer People would
come.
The Old One came softly.
She was heavy with a fawn.
She had old scars from the Wolf People.

She came to us
and talked to me.
"We know you, tsimmu.
Thank you for the gift."

She looked long at me
and I stalked her
as she watched.

Those last days are hard as we hike back to the Jeep. When we arrive it is very early morning. Mike tried to scare Mckenzie back into the forest, away from us, but she still follows me. She thinks I will stay with her. Mike gets into his truck and drives some distance to wait. She noses around the area where the Jeep is parked. I stand nearby and watch silently, sensing her wilderness. This may be the last time I see the Gray One so I savor the moments, watch and feel for her decision. At last, I call Mckenzie to me and open the car door. The woman's eyes, amber brown, and the wolf's eyes, yellow gold, meet—-earth and sunlight. "You choose, Baby, stay or go. If you get in the car I will take you back with me. But you will always be captive. We might still go hunting but you will not live the life that The Mystery intended for you. You choose for yourself. I can't go with you. I've been a wolf for a while, now I must be a human being."

Mckenzie, whose name is fading from her the way a wolf shakes water from its coat, jumps into the Jeep. She smells the odors of her friends, Beanie and Peter, like she is reading a book. Then she jumps out again and with one wild serious look, our spirits touch. She then runs off towards the mountains where the old doe lies on the ground waiting to give life.

My drive home is the long way, through roads and spirit paths. I live lifetimes driving home without Mckenzie thinking of her by herself in the mountains. I know her life will be shorter than if she had stayed with me. Mckenzie does not fear death, but captivity. And so do I. For a long time I struggled with my questions and drank at the bitter spring. Wolf With No Name. What is Freedom? What is Wilderness? What is Captivity? What is Domestication? The answer is the singing of wolves who call to the pack, who live for each other. And from horses who let me sit on them and carry me over fences without bridle or saddle. They, too, live for each other. And they do not build walls. The wolves and horses know how to grow and live and not be frightened in their bodies.

Five days later Mike and I drive out of the brush and stop at an espresso stand to get coffee. Weekday-morning people dressed in their good clothes eat lunch away from their work. They stare at us as the dog stares at the wolf. We are wild. We then walk back to the car and drive into the cage.

Sixty days later the pain in my heart has not lessened. Then one morning the phone rings. It is my friend Linda.

"T, I saw your wolf on TV."

"What? I don't want to hear this. Was it the Department of Fish and Game?"

"Take it easy," Linda says calmly. "Two biologists saw her. They think she's native. They took photos from a distance."

I get up my nerve to call Frank. I tell him that I am a college student doing wolf research.

"There was a pair sighted in the mountains, indigenous," offers Frank.

"Yes? What colors are they?"

"Light gray, and dark."

My heart beats somewhere between excitement and fear. "Do they look fit?" "

Yes, skinny but it's still early spring. We're going to try to tag them."

My heart alternately sinks and leaps in joy. She is alive and has found another wolf! But they will go and tag her. I dislike that and decide I will go back to the mountains and take the collar away if they tag her. A radio collar! How pompous to think that this will not interfere with her life. The best way to study wildlife is to go and quietly watch. It takes a lot longer, but the knowledge is pure and not tainted. There is a saying that if you try to gain knowledge by using cruelty, then the knowledge is perverted and this is not wisdom. The radio collar would be cruel for Mckenzie. I send thoughts to her. *Stay hidden. Stay away from people.*

That first summer without her my heart breaks missing her. Every day I wonder, *What is she doing now? Hunting? Searching the trails with the other wolf? Does she call to me?* Some evenings I fancied I could hear her howling in her sweet wild voice. Perhaps she thinks of us close by hunting. I call Frank several times and pray he will not dart her to get the collar on. I know how that will affect her. I know how it would affect me.

I wait till fall so as to give Mckenzie a chance to get used to life without me. I also want to go back to find her when there are only a few people in the park.

Alone, I return to the mountains, fall is approaching. The border guards do not want me to hike into the mountains by myself and frown at my lack of gear. "You can't possibly camp in those parts by yourself," they advise. "I'm meeting someone," I tell them. They somehow find this believable and let me pass. Yes I am meeting someone—my daughter.

I camp by the little lake that I named, "Sounds Like a Bear" and I hear the sounds of logging right next to the park. I want to howl to Mckenzie and call her down to me, but the loggers keep me silent. Peter is with me and we hike the trails together. Coming up out of deep brush we stumble upon two men with a poached elk. I appear almost right under them and it gives all of us a terrible start. I run. They call after me and chase me for a short distance but Peter and I lose them.

My tears wet the land where she walks. I grieve that I will not see her. We finally settle down in the brush to sleep. My dreams in the wilderness are pleasant, wrapped in warmth. The wind sighs above me and my troubled memory is erased in the blessing that sleep gives. There is a point in the morning that is forever, it is the pearly moment before sunrise. The birds are few this time of year but I hear a jay screech once and I feel the wind move softly over my bare face.

Something is curled next to me, breathing in my ear, and chewing softly on my pants leg. Slowly, I put my arm out and feel not the short coat of Peter, but the long guard hairs of a form I know well. Fully awake with a start, the impossible sweetness in my heart does not dare to hope that it could be her. The body snuggled so gently against me jumps up and climbs the little hillside nearby. Peter stands beside me slow-

ly wagging his tail. I lift my eyes and look over my shoulder, the wind pulls my hair sharp like the playful nips of wolves.

It is Mckenzie. I call to her, "Baby?" Her ears prick up and she flicks her white tail. How tall she is! And there is a wisdom in her eyes, a maturity. Gone is her awkwardness. She is an adult, a person, a being living in her world. But now she is wild and her people call her. She pants her greeting, then turns and disappears into the brush. I take my pony bead necklace and leave half the beads there, a gift for the deer.

For a long time Peter and I watch the brush where she disappeared. I wonder what her mate thought. The wolf who had accepted her and helped her back home. Did he wonder at her foolishness? Soon I realize that we are done here. Always I will return to this spot and I know Mckenzie will know that autumn is the gathering time for her first family. Now it is time for me to go home to the island.

The next spring hiking close to those same mountains, I

meet a ranger posting a sign. The sign states that this is a delicate wildlife area and no longer open to hikers. "Why?" I ask. The ranger smiles. "I'm not supposed to tell anyone, but there is a wolf den here." The wolf is endangered and they want to protect the den from people. I look him dead in the eye. My turn to smile.

For a long time after Mckenzie's release, I feel her. In my mind, I see her lying in the sun after a good hunt or on a snowy day trailing game. I hear her voice swinging through the fir trees all the way to the island. But after a while the feeling is less, almost like a campfire dwindling down through the night.

I know she thought of me especially when I did not come back the second autumn after her release. I felt she probably went back to the first camp, but finding me absent, went back to the mountains. I had to restrain myself from distracting her from her life. I was afraid of drawing attention to her. She and I had to let go. Does she look for me? Her howling rings in my bones.

Daughter.

Grandfather, what a price I am paying,
grieving over one who is my sister, now not seen.
She would run before me, joyful,
then turn and look; still coming, you!

I taught her how to take life for food,
life for living. I had to honor these ones.
I cannot go back,
I cannot see her captive, yet now I cannot see her.

Do you understand, Gray One?
Did you choose? I wonder.
I left you and I feel like you're betrayed.
But I'm betrayed.

We are neither one thing nor the other.
I envy you your journey,
though it may be short.
I wish I could follow, I did see wolf sign.
Please find your family,
please find your food,
please find your life and sing;
sing for the one in the cabin who couldn't come.

Grandfather walks.
He comes to me and we look out in the gray.
We see wolves,
wolves
then only trees.

Epilogue

It has been more than six years since Mckenzie and I parted. She may be dead. Life as a free person can be very short, but it is what you do with the life you have, not how long you live it.

On my last birthday, I found a young wild duck hanging upside down from a briar bush. Her foot was caught in the spines, and she dangled by her two feet above the brown pond water. Her mother swam close by, muttering confused and pitiful sounds. I could feel emotion, thick like honey, pouring from her voice.

Wading to the little duck and releasing her, I could see she was unable to move. She had a large sore on her back. I took her into my home and put salve on her wound, then placed her in a box with a light to keep her from freezing.

After a couple of hours she was moving normally. I put her in my shower stall and gave her water and food. When my hand was down near the duck arranging things, she nuzzled up against it like it was familiar. She used her little bill to pry between my fingers for warmth, making soft cheeping sounds.

In that moment, I held the earth in my hands. The earth looked like a wild migratory water bird staring at me with black sharp shiny eyes. We are vulnerable and not quite alone, even when we think we are. Animals feel. We are all the same in that everything dies to life. The Mystery lives all around us.

That night I dreamed I stood on the Plains calling Mckenzie. I stood next to Cherry the red Jeep on an old road and called and called. The Gray One came, but now she could fly. She circled me like the west wind, so close the current of her flight rustled her feathers, and I could hear them. Mckenzie, my daughter the wolf, was an eagle.

We dive back and forth through time like dolphins. Leap up in the sunlight with the spray shining where we can see each other; dive down into darkness where blue thoughts swim. We all are one.

One year after Mckenzie's release, I was busy promoting my first book, *Learning from Eagle, Living with Coyote*. The bookstore owners who hosted the reading gave me a gift, a book about the wildlife in the wilderness area where Mckenzie was released. There is no way that the bookstore people could have known that. Turning the pages I came to photographs. One photo caught up my heart like a leaf in the wind. It is the Gray One. She is trotting and looks thin,

but very much alive. I read the book and found that because of Mckenzie's sighting and the sighting of a grizzly, the area may be made into an international peace park.

I called my mother to tell her of the incidents that synchronicity brought to me. She said that God is trying to tell me that Mckenzie is all right. Mother had gone to church during the final release and stood up and asked the congregation to pray for her daughter who was looking for a pack of wolves in the mountains. The church had prayed and so had the land. Were people praying for me then? Are people praying now? I feel them the way I feel stars above me in the daylight.

Lev and Teresa and Cherry.

Soon after Mckenzie's release a man gave me an adult wolf. I call him Lev. He is not very predatory and is too old to learn the life that the Gray One lives. But I take Lev and Peter and Beanie to the Blackfeet Nation and there find balance for my unsteady feet.

In a lonely gas station overlooking the golden-green Plains, where the grass bends gently in the dance with the little wind, cars drive up and families get out. They ask to be introduced to the wolves. "We are related," they say. They gently pet Lev who is tame, then leave, smiling. And as I stare out over the grassland my heart melts and I cry. There are wolves here and people will not shoot them because they are connected like kin.

Far from the wilderness or maybe closer than you think, listen to the blood in your veins, you belong to Earth, you are wild. The Gray One gives you a gift, she gives you her name.

And she asks you, hunting with piercing yellow eyes, *Do you know your relatives?*

Look for me in the north. I still go to the mountains. I have family there and so do we all. The Wolf People teach us to hunt and care for our kin. The Singing People guard the game to keep them strong.

Our teachers and partners, the guides and the guardians, call us. We are invited back to Coyote's campfire to belong again, to sit on our Mother's lap and be Natives of the land.

Teresa tsimmu Martino
1996

Photo: Nancy Clendaniel

Teresa with Peter and Lev.

About the Author

Teresa tsimmu Martino is the daughter of a first-generation Italian-American father, and a mother of Osage and Scots-Irish descent. Her middle name, tsimmu, was given to her by a Native man from her childhood. It is derived from the Yumi word that means "dreams of a wolf."

She lives on an island in the Pacific Northwest where she writes, paints and sculpts, and works as a horse trainer. She began riding horses when she was four years old and has been working as a professional trainer for more than twenty-one years. Martino lives with three wolves, Peter, Shoka and Lev, and her companion dog of twelve years, Beanie. She also has done wolf rescue work.

Her first book is a volume of stories and poetry, *Learning from Eagle, Living with Coyote* (Orion Books, 1993). She is at present completing two new books: *Dancer on the Grass*, stories about horses and people (NewSage Press, Fall 1997); and *Trick from the Sky, Wind Like Horse Hair* (NewSage Press) a story about family, ancestry, and myth. For information on her art work, contact the author at: PO Box 13115, Burton, WA 98013.

Books by NewSage Press

Animals as Teachers & Healers: True Stories & Reflections
Susan Chernak McElroy
(NewSage book available from Ballantine Books in 1997)

Council of the Animals: Wisdom for Healing the Earth
Story by Michael W. Fox
Illustrations by Susan Seddon Boulet & Michael McNelly
(March 1997)

Eating with Conscience: The Bioethics of Food
Michael W. Fox (April 1997)

One Woman, One Vote: Rediscovering the Woman Suffrage Movement
Edited by Marjorie Spruill Wheeler

Jailed for Freedom: American Women Win the Vote
Doris Stevens, Edited by Carol O'Hare

Women & Work: In Their Own Words
Edited by Maureen R. Michelson

Blue Moon Over Thurman Street
Ursula K. Le Guin
Photographs by Roger Dorband

When the Bough Breaks: Pregnancy & the Legacy of Addiction
Kira Corser & Frances Payne Adler

A Portrait of American Mothers & Daughters
Raisa Fastman

Organizing for Our Lives: New Voices from Rural Communities
Richard Steven Street & Samuel Orozco

Family Portraits in Changing Times
Helen Nestor

Stories of Adoption: Loss & Reunion
Eric Blau, M.D.

Common Heroes: Facing a Life Threatening Illness
Eric Blau, M.D.

For a catalog contact NewSage Press, PO Box 607, Troutdale, OR 97060
Phone (503) 695-2211 Fax (503) 695-5406